OSPREY MASTERCLASS

Armour Modelling

John Prigent
Series editors Marcus Cowper and Nikolai Bogdanŏvic

First published in Great Britain in 2006 by Osprey Publishing,
PO Box 883, Oxford, OX1 9PL, UK
PO Box 3985, New York, NY 10185-3985, USA
Email: info@ospreypublishing.com

Osprey Publishing is part of the Osprey Group.

© 2006 Osprey Publishing Ltd.

All rights reserved. Apart from any fair dealing for the purpose of private study,
research, criticism or review, as permitted under the Copyright, Designs and
Patents Act, 1988, no part of this publication may be reproduced, stored in
a retrieval system, or transmitted in any form or by any means, electronic,
electrical, chemical, mechanical, optical, photocopying, recording or otherwise,
without the prior written permission of the copyright owner. Enquiries should
be addressed to the Publishers.

A CIP catalogue record for this book is available from the British Library

ISBN 978 1 84176 974 5

Page layout by Ken Vail Graphic Design (www.kvgd.com)
Index by Alison Worthington
Typeset in Stone Sans and Centaur MT
Originated by United Graphics, Singapore
Printed and bound in China through World Print Ltd.

13 14 15 16 17   16 15 14 13 12 11 10 9 8 7

The Woodland Trust
Osprey Publishing is supporting the Woodland Trust, the UK's leading
woodland conservation charity, by funding the dedication of trees.

www.ospreypublishing.com

CONTENTS

		Foreword	4
		Introduction	5
■	Chapter 1	Tools, materials and paint	6
■	Chapter 2	Building Dragon's initial Tiger	14
■	Chapter 3	More painting and finishing ideas and simple improvements	32
■	Chapter 4	The basics of bases	48
■	Chapter 5	Working with etched metal	60
■	Chapter 6	Kits with resin and white-metal parts	74
■	Chapter 7	A simple scratch-built conversion	92
■	Chapter 8	Hotchkiss Geschützwagen	104
■	Chapter 9	Sturmgeschütz IV	126
■	Chapter 10	IDF Tiran 5 Main Battle Tank	152
■	Chapter 11	References and research	174
■	Chapter 12	Sources	180
		Index	188

Foreword

It was around nearly 60 years ago that a very much younger John Prigent cut up his empty breakfast cereal box for the cardboard to make himself a model tank. He reckons a British Matilda infantry tank was the result and, since then, progressively with more modern materials, his interest in modelling military vehicles, and the real thing, hasn't waned.

It is said that everyone has a book in them – including modellers – but writing a book isn't easy, especially one about model making for what is obviously a niche interest. Not everyone can do it, usually due to the inability of finding publishers willing to produce books for what is a very specialized market. Another reason is that not everyone possesses all the relevant skills necessary: building the models, photographing the progress of the build from beginning to end, showing techniques used in an instructional step-by-step style, and just simply writing about how to do it.

In the 1990s John was responsible for writing a series in *Military Modelling* magazine called the 'Tank Modelling Course', where he took readers from the very beginnings of building a plastic kit, through kit conversions and on to building parts and models from scratch. We've moved on somewhat since then and the update of the information in these articles forms the core for this, John's first book for Osprey about making models of military vehicles in which he passes on his experiences and the techniques he's learned and developed over the years.

He's also invited some Osprey author friends to contribute further material on different techniques to complete the picture, following the natural route from essential tools and materials through basic kit building to more advanced conversions. Unlike other titles in the Osprey modelling series that concentrate on single subject types or series, John's book follows the general modelling route, making it the ideal primer for anyone new to the hobby of modelling miniature military vehicles.

Ken Jones

INTRODUCTION

I have been a model builder for nearly 60 years, using many different materials and methods. My first was a Matilda tank, made in 1947 with cardboard cut from breakfast cornflake boxes, but as well as tanks I have built models ranging from aircraft carved in sections from solid balsa wood to large-scale cars and full-rigged sailing ships. Many of the methods I used are still the same for 21st-century plastic models; even the carving of balsa wood prepared me to shape new parts from solid plastic! Some years ago, because there had been many comments from newcomers to model building that no-one explained the techniques they needed to know to handle the increasing number of etched-metal and resin accessories and conversions appearing on the market, I wrote for *Military Modelling* magazine a series called the 'Tank Modelling Course' aimed specifically to meet their needs.

Now Osprey has asked me to revise and update it, and here is the result. It's not just for beginners, we show many methods that advanced and master level modellers use so if you've already built some models you can use this book to move up to those levels yourself.

In two respects it is quite unlike the series – first, none of the material used there is repeated and, second, this time I have asked some of my friends to contribute special chapters showing techniques that they are expert in. In other ways it is very much the same, starting with the most basic ideas and moving up to quite advanced techniques with explanations of how to do everything. Here you will find 'how to' hints to answer all the questions that I and my friends could think of, from how to take parts off their moulding trees to the basics of scratch-building. My friends and I take you through the building of a selection of models using not just the original plastic parts, but also aftermarket accessories in etched metal, turned metal gun barrels, resin conversions and accessories, and scratch-built parts using a variety of materials; it also includes how to paint and weather them as well as make scenic bases. The models are 'demonstrators' for the methods you need to build any model so don't think you have to make the same kits as us – just read how we built them and apply the same methods. They will work just as well for aircraft, car or train models, too.

I'd like to give special thanks here to Nick Cortese, Gary Edmundson and Steve Zaloga for contributing their special chapters as well as to Ken Jones for agreeing to write a Foreword. I must also thank the manufacturers and retailers who helped so much by furnishing kits and tools for the book and rushing my orders to me: Accurate Armour, Archer Fine Transfers, Dragon Models Ltd, Formations, Historex Agents, K59, LSA Models, Michigan Discount Models, Mission Models, R&J Enterprises and The Small Shop EU.

Extra special thanks go to my wife Joan for her understanding and support while I worked on the book, as well as for providing frequent cups of tea when I was concentrating so hard that I forgot to drink them until they'd gone cold!

So without more ado, turn the page for the first chapter on choosing tools and paints for your first model.

John Prigent

Tools, materials and paint

To build any model you are going to need some simple tools and some paints, so let's look at them. A knife, files, adhesive, filler putty and paint and brushes are the basics, and a small drill is very useful. They're all discussed here or later in the book, when you need them for particular jobs.

The basic toolkit

The first thing to get is a hobby knife. There are several different kinds, with either built-in blades, interchangeable blades or blades that you can snap off as you go to keep a sharp tip.

I do not recommend the ones with a built-in blade. You have to pay for a new handle every time you need a sharp new blade, and it is difficult to dispose of the old one safely.

My personal favourite is the type with interchangeable blades. There are several kinds but I have used X-Acto and Excel knives and blades for many years, so I can recommend them both. Both makes' handles and blades fit each other, which is very handy if you run out of blades and only the 'other ones' are easy to find where you live! There are three sizes of handle, numbered 1, 2 and 3 for light, medium and heavy work respectively; I find that a No. 1 will do most jobs, so I suggest you get this one. Both makers offer a variety of blades to fit each handle. I use the long-pointed, single-edged No. 11 blades for almost everything and this is the one you should get; they come in packs of five so buy a spare pack at the same time as buying the No. 1 handle they fit (which usually comes with a blade provided). A No. 17 chisel blade fits the same handle and is very handy for some jobs, so a pack of those as well will set you up for quite a while. The saw blade I favour is made by both X-Acto and Excel and has a solid backing strip that fits into a No. 3 handle. This handle is something extra to buy, so it is worth looking at the saw blades sold by other manufacturers that fit the No. 1 handle. All of these blades are secured to their handles by knurled sleeves that screw down over a collet that holds the blade, so there's no risk of the blade coming loose or slipping unless you're very careless fitting it. There are other types of knife with interchangeable and replaceable blades, so choose whatever fits your hand best and will be easiest to use. Whatever you buy, keep the box or tube that your spare blades come in – you will need it to store them safely.

A cutting mat with knives and spare blades; the saw blade needs a larger handle that isn't shown here.

A selection of useful files and their cleaning brush. The diamond files on the left are good for delicate work.

though a set of small modelling files is always handy because there are some jobs that only they can tackle, like smoothing down the last bit of excess plastic at a joint. I actually have two sets: one provides the half-inch-wide, flat file that I use most and a second contains fine, diamond files, including several round and shaped ones for tricky areas. A copper-wire suede brush will remove filing dust from their teeth. Many modellers find it simpler and cheaper to buy 'sanding sticks' instead of files – these are basically lollipop sticks with fine sandpaper on each side, but you do have to throw them away when the sandpaper starts to wear away. Tweezers will also be useful for holding small parts so that they can be painted or cemented in place. I do not recommend the 'self-closing' ones with sprung ends that you open by squeezing the tweezers. 'Tweezer launch' is something you'll hear about from many modellers, and happens when a small part slips from your tweezers because it's held too tightly.

JOINING THE PARTS – GLUES, CEMENTS AND PUTTIES

Special glues are made for polystyrene plastic, the kind used in most model kits, and these 'plastic cements' come in two types: fairly

The third type of knife has a blade that slides inside its handle and is held by a knob on the handle's side. When the tip gets blunt you simply loosen the screw, slide the blade out a bit and break off the tip at a line engraved on the blade. This gives you a new sharp tip and cutting edge. You can do this quite a few times before you need a new knife, but you must be careful snapping off the old tip – use pliers, or wear leather gloves, to avoid accidentally cutting yourself. The tips of these knives are quite hard to get into tight places, but some modellers find them very useful so do consider them while you're looking to see which knife suits you.

Next on the shopping list is a cutting mat. These are self-healing, so when you cut something on them your blade won't leave a slit behind it as you would on a wooden or plastic surface. Even with this protection whatever surface you work on will deserve care, so I suggest a cheap tray or an old drawing board. I use a drawing board myself, covered with an old newspaper to protect it from spilt glue and paint. This lets me simply throw away the newspaper when it gets cluttered by bits of cut-off plastic or smeared with that paint and glue – but be careful not to throw away model parts with it! The other advantage of a tray or board is that you can simply pick it up and move it to tidy up at the end of a modelling session or when the table is needed for something else.

I do most of my modelling work with just this simple equipment – a knife, cutting mat, and board,

Here is a collection of typical cements and glues, with the superglue debonder.

thick, in a tube like toothpaste, and fairly thin, in a bottle. Both types work by melting the plastic so that parts are welded together.

Most tube cements are fairly slow drying, so you have time to adjust the parts you are cementing together. You use them by squeezing the tube as you run its nozzle along a joint surface before putting the parts together. They can fill any gaps where parts do not quite meet properly at a joint, but they are hard to control – squeeze too hard and you get too much cement in the joint, which will make a blob on your model and leave a mark that can be hard to hide. Some of these cements come in a squeezy plastic bottle with a metal applicator tube built into it. These are a bit runnier, so easier to control, but you will still need to be careful not to apply too much to the joint.

The thin, liquid cements are applied with a brush, usually to parts that are already held together by your fingers but you can brush them onto a joining surface and press the part into place instead. They evaporate quickly, so the second method will only work on small parts – by the time you have applied cement all along a long joint the start of it will be dry again. Many manufacturers offer these, almost all with a brush

Model fillers. The tube variety must have its cap on when not in use, and although I've removed the two parts of the epoxy filler from their wrapper to show you, they must be kept wrapped when not in use or they will mix where they touch and be spoilt. Sometimes epoxy filler goes hard when it's been kept for a long time, but this is just a surface skin that you can cut off to find good epoxy under it.

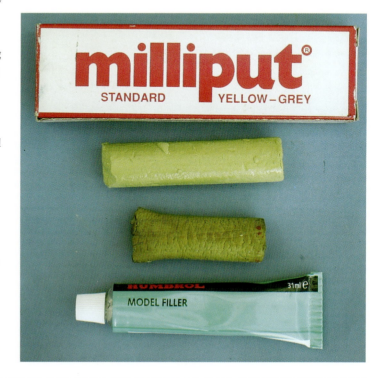

> **Warning:** younger modellers should not use superglues without an adult nearby to help out, and like all glues you must remember not to hold the tube near your eyes to squeeze it – all glues have fumes that will make your eyes sore if too close to them, and superglue can actually cement your eyelids together.

provided in the bottle-top. The difference between them is the degree of 'runniness' that allows the cement to seep between the parts to be joined. The main thing to be careful about is that the built-in brush is too thick to run along a joint without spreading cement beyond it. That is fine if you can put the cement on the inside where it will not be seen, but if you have to apply it on the outside, where it will show, you need to use a finer brush. We'll look at brushes in a moment.

There are also cyanoacrylate cements, usually known as superglues or crazy glues. Here also there are two basic kinds, thick and thin. Both dry quickly and can stick skin, so take care not to get them on yourself. They are essential for joining metal or resin parts together, or to plastic; but don't use them for joining plastic parts together until you are thoroughly used to them. When you buy superglue look for 'debonder' too – it will dissolve any mistaken joints, sticking a part to your finger perhaps, and also let you separate stuck fingers from each other.

You will often find that, no matter how careful you are in building a model, there are tiny gaps between some of its parts. In order to fill these you will need the tubes labelled 'model filler' or 'model putty' on your hobby shop's rack, generally near the cements and paints. There are two kinds: simple putties in a tube and two-part epoxy putties, like the famous Milliput, that you have to mix together. The simple tube putty will do for most jobs, and is obviously easier to use than anything you have to mix, but it can shrink as it dries and need a second application to get a smooth surface. Like anything else in a tube, the cap must not be left off or it will dry out. The two-part putties do not shrink and produce a good surface, but they harden when mixed so leftovers cannot be kept for use later. This simply means that you should only mix as much as you need for each job. The separate parts need to be kept in their wrappers and may eventually develop a 'skin', but this does not matter. I have kept both kinds of putty for years, using a bit at a time, and found them still good

after five years so you need not worry about them going out of date.

PAINT AND BRUSHES

There are several kinds of paint for models – enamel, acrylic and lacquer – as well as varieties specially formulated for use in an airbrush and the ones that come in spray cans. All should be applied in thin coats to avoid covering the details of your model. Most model paints will cover cleanly with a single coat, but red, yellow and white often need more than one. Enamels, acrylics or lacquers can be painted over each other without harm, so a coat of white acrylic spray will give a good undercoat before you use the main colours.

Most enamel paints come in small tins, and there is a very wide variety of colours available. Humbrol, Revell and Tamiya are the most common brands, and are compatible with each other – you can mix different makers' enamels to get the shade of colour that you want, and once the first coat is dry you can paint them over each other without any problems. You need a special thinner to clean your brushes after using enamels, and all the enamel manufacturers offer their own thinners as well. All seem to be exactly the same, so you don't need to match the thinner to the paint if you use more than one brand of enamel. The thinners usually come in small bottles, so

Enamel and acrylic paints with the enamel thinner – acrylic paints are thinned and cleaned up with water – and my recommended selection of brushes.

start with one of these but don't throw it away when it's empty. Refill it from one of the large cans of thinner that good hobby shops have on their shelves and save money! Do avoid the enamels that you'll find in car accessory shops: they are not the same as modelling paints and some may damage the plastic, though acrylic car paints are okay to use.

Acrylic paints are water based, so brushes can be cleaned with soap and water. Tamiya, Gunze Sangyo, Humbrol, Vallejo Model Color, Games Workshop's Citadel, Lifecolor and Andrea are common brands. They offer an even wider range of colours than enamels. Some may not be compatible if you try to mix them, but you can experiment to find out. One problem I have found with some acrylics is that a second brushed coat can 'drag' at the first coat and spoils it, which is rather inconvenient if it is one of the colours that needs more than one coat to provide complete coverage of the plastic.

Lacquers are mostly found from Gunze Sangyo, though there are other makers. Again, there's a wide range of colours but you need 'cellulose' thinners to clean your brush. These are sold for the 'dope' used on flying model aircraft, so most hobby shops have them.

As a final option you can use watercolours, gouache or poster paints for some jobs. They clean up with soap and water like acrylics, and they can be very handy for some things as you'll see in one of the modelling chapters.

Whatever paint and thinner you choose, never dip your brush in the bottle of thinner as it just makes the thinner dirty! Tip some into a small container, like the top of a yoghurt pot, and clean your brush in that. Test the container

These are typical spray cans. The Tamiya spray is a lacquer that can be cleaned with cellulose thinners that you can buy in any shop that sells materials for flying model aircraft, and the Citadel is acrylic.

by leaving some thinner in it for a while, because thinners tend to melt through some plastics so you need to check that this will not happen and change your container if necessary. The ideal container is the metal pot that many artists use for thinners; look in an art shop for one.

Brushes also come in a wide choice. You can get sable hair, pig's hair, squirrel hair and various synthetic hairs in several different qualities, as well as many different shapes and sizes. What you should avoid is buying the cheap 'modeller's brushes' that you'll find in most hobby shops: they deteriorate too quickly and lose their points – if they have points in the first place. They are useful for some things, though, so buy a thin one for applying the liquid cement to put your model together. Mark it in some way so you only use this one for cement, your 'painting' brushes don't need cement on them! Buy your brushes for proper painting at an artists' shop, but not the top quality ones as model paints are a lot harder on the bristles than artists' oil colours. Look for students' brushes instead. The basic shapes are Filbert (flattish with a rounded tip), Flat (wide and flat), Round (comes to a tip) and Rigger (has a definite

Parts that feel 'greasy'

You will occasionally find that the parts you're handling feel 'greasy'. This is because all moulds need a release agent so the parts will come out of them easily. Most of these agents don't stay on the parts, but sometimes they do leave a coating. Even if it is not noticeable, get rid of it because it will stop paint adhering properly to your model. Rinse the parts in warm, not hot, water with a little washing-up liquid. Pat them as dry as you can on kitchen paper and let them finish drying by themselves. Don't try to accelerate drying by putting them in front of a fire or in a warm, sunny window, or with a hairdryer: the plastic will melt!

A selection of various brushes allows the modeller to apply paint to a wide range of surfaces on armour models and figures. Smaller size 000 to 1 brushes are used for details like vehicle tools, tyres and figure's faces. The wider brushes cover bigger tasks. The widest type shown is handy for dry-brushing jobs, using very small amounts of paint pigment.

point). The Rigger was designed to paint fine lines, like lettering or the rigging in paintings of ships, so this and the Round are good choices. Ask if you can damp the brush tips (many art shops will find you a pot of water for this) to check how good their points are, especially important for the Riggers. The sizes are numbered from 0000 upwards with the higher numbers being progressively thicker. I recommend 000, 1 and perhaps 2 in Riggers to make it easier to paint small parts, the faces of crew figures, and fine details; and a Round 3 for the main painting of your model's camouflage.

You will have noticed that I didn't mention spray cans with the rest of the paints. That is because they need no brushes and no thinners! They are especially useful for undercoats, white interiors and single-colour camouflage finishes. I have only used those from Citadel and Tamiya, but they all work exactly the same way. Start a bit to the side of your model or part and sweep gently across it from about 30cm away – if you start spraying directly onto the model, or too close, any foam or blob inside the can will end up on the model and spoil its finish. When you are done, turn the can upside-down and spray until the stream from the nozzle has no paint in it. Finally, wipe the nozzle with kitchen paper and replace the cap on the can.

An airbrush is an expensive tool, whether you buy a compressor for it or use 'canned air'. I do not recommend that you buy one for your first models, keep your money for the essentials mentioned above instead.

All paints need to be stirred thoroughly before use, or shaken hard if they're in bottles or spray cans whose lids you can't take off. Don't use a brush as a stirrer! Instead, look around for a suitable metal rod that you can wipe clean every time it is used. A better alternative is Tamiya's cheap set of two stirrers with a flat face at one end and a small spoon at the other. They are ideal because as well as stirring with them you can use the 'spoon' end to measure drops of paint when you need to mix colours.

The main paint makers include in their ranges colours that are listed as matches for the main German and US camouflage colours. Unfortunately, some of these matches are far from accurate. My friends and I will consider the actual colours of paint needed as we describe the models, but for the moment what you need to know is that some kits also have misleading colours listed on their instructions. For instance, if you see 'field grey' mentioned as the colour for a German tank you should actually be looking for 'tank grey' or 'panzer grey' unless your hobby shop carries the actual paint number in the range quoted by the instructions. This is because field grey and panzer grey are completely different colours, and the specific 'field grey' with that number in that maker's range is actually panzer grey – probably a translation problem. Many tank colours are not covered by any maker whose paints can easily be found in hobby shops, so for them you will need to resort to mixing colours or to mail order (see the chapter listing sources for suppliers).

A QUESTION OF SCALE

As you look at hobby shop shelves you'll see several 'scales' marked on the boxes, mostly 1/72, 1/48 and 1/35. There are many other possibilities, but to understand them all you need to know is that they represent the ratio of model size to the real thing – in other words, at 1/35 scale 1in. represents 35in. on a real tank, and 1mm equals 35mm. In this book 1/35-scale kits have been used because they allow all the techniques to be shown without making the detail pictures too small to be useful, but you can use the methods described on kits at any scale.

EXTRA TOOLS FOR OTHER JOBS

You are going to find occasions when you need to keep paint off places on your model, perhaps because you want to spray or airbrush parts before assembly. For this you need masking tape. Tamiya makes a very good low-tack tape that does not pull paint away from completed areas. It is available in most good hobby shops and comes in several widths. You can also buy 'frisket', or masking sheet, from artists' shops. This is good to use for special shapes – you can even draw a marking on it and carefully cut out the parts that need paint to make your own special painting mask. Check how sticky it is by painting a bit of plastic with your base colour and rubbing the frisket onto it once it is dry. Then pull the frisket away – if paint comes with it you will need to reduce its sticking power. Just rub your new mask onto your cutting mat and pull it away again, then do the test again.

From time to time you will need to drill holes. Here you have the choice between a battery-powered small electric mini-drill – Dremel is probably the best-known make – and a tiny hand-drill called a 'pin vice'. The electric drill is very good for major jobs but it does have some drawbacks. First, you need to make sure the one you buy has a variable speed control, because too high a speed can make your drill bit melt the plastic you're drilling into! You also need to have a very steady hand while you use it, in order not to let the bit 'bounce' across the surface and make a misshapen hole or one where you don't want it. The third factor is cost, though small battery-powered drills are not too expensive. While you are learning new techniques it's best to keep your equipment as simple as possible, and you can do most jobs with a pin vice so that's what I recommend. It's very light, so easy to hold and control, and its speed is entirely dependent on you

because you turn it between your fingers.

With it you will need some drill bits. Get a set with sizes from 0.5 to 2mm, and it is handy to pick up spares of the smallest sizes because they are surprisingly easy to break. A set of shaped-head rotary rasps will make a useful purchase too; mine are diamond-coated and let me make indentations of various shapes for such jobs as opening holes to fit proper reflectors into headlights.

When you are ready to use etched-metal detailing sets you will need some extra tools. At the very least you will want a small pair of smooth-jawed pliers, to hold parts while you clean them, and a 150mm steel ruler – you'll find the ruler very useful for other things too. You don't need special scissors to cut etched parts from their fret, your knife blade will do. There are some special tools for bending and curving etched-metal parts that are described later.

BUILDING DRAGON'S INITIAL TIGER

The Tiger is one of the most popular tank modelling subjects and it's not hard to see why – the real tank is famous, it was built with many variations so you can make many models with no two quite the same, it is big and impressive with a correspondingly impressive gun and, being a German tank, it has many possible colour schemes. This makes it very popular among modellers and therefore also with kit manufacturers.

When I started writing this book Dragon Models Ltd (DML for short) had just announced a 1/35-scale kit of the very first production variant so it was an obvious choice for the first build! Thanks to my friend Ken Jones, DML provided an early sample for me to start work, and I'd like to thank both Ken and Freddie Leung of DML for this.

This kit offers offers optional parts, several colour schemes and a host of alternative parts in both plastic and etched metal. The large box has an attractive illustration on the top and lots of detail photographs on the sides and bottom, so you can see what you're buying.

ALWAYS STUDY THE INSTRUCTIONS FIRST

The first thing to do with any kit is to study the instructions and identify all the parts. Yes, obvious I know, but you'll hear even expert modellers saying 'when all else fails, read the instructions'. This reflects

the temptation to assume that having read them once you can just go ahead and assemble parts that 'look as if they fit together'. Quite often there are several parts that look very similar, and this is why all good kits have letters to identify the 'sprues' – the moulding trees that the parts are attached to – and numbers on the sprues beside each part. The instructions show the same letters and numbers, so if they say X25 against the next part you need to fit you must find sprue X and part 25 on it.

But this is not completely foolproof! Sometimes there are misprints on an instruction sheet, but you can identify these because X25 simply doesn't fit where it should. Always 'dry fit' – place parts together without cement – to check before doing anything permanent. This also lets you see whether location pins and their holes, meant to help line parts up properly, do actually match. Sometimes you'll need to deepen a hole before its pin can fit, or to cut off a pin that is in the wrong

place. But be careful to check first that you do have the correct two parts! I have sometimes found myself trying to fit the wrong part so you need not worry if you make that mistake. This kit does not have any of those problems, but think about them if you build a different model.

CONSIDER THE OPTIONS

Now it's time to think about the options in the kit and decide which of them to use. This kit gives optional open or closed positions for hatches; plastic or metal for some parts; and also alternative stowage boxes to go on the turret depending on the colour scheme and markings you like. Once you have decided take a pencil and cross out the parts you do not want to use in all the instructions' illustrations. This can mean crossing out complete illustrations when an option is shown as an assembly by itself, but don't forget to cross out the place where that assembly is fitted.

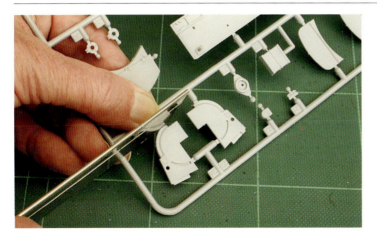

TOP Some modellers use side cutters to remove parts, but it is safest to use a razor saw.

BOTTOM You can also cut parts free with a knife, but keep them flat on the cutting board while you do it and hold tiny ones with a finger so they don't get lost.

modellers use side cutters — special tools similar to wire cutters — but these can also bend or break small parts so I advise using your knife or saw instead. I prefer my saw for most parts, but sometimes there simply isn't room to get it into place without damaging either the part I need or one next to it. Support the sprue with one hand and spread your fingers to hold the part as well. Then gently saw through where the part connects to the sprue, but not right next to the part. Some parts have their connections against delicate areas,

You also need to think about how you will paint the parts – some are best painted before assembly. Most kit instructions have you fixing wheels and tracks in place at an early stage, but with this Tiger it's going to be hard to paint in between the wheels once they're stuck together, and hard to paint the hull behind them, so I suggest that you keep them as individual parts till they and the hull are painted.

REMOVING THE PARTS FROM THEIR SPRUES

Now you're ready to start assembly. The first thing needed is to take the parts off their sprues. It is tempting to simply twist them till they come away, but this will usually either leave a bit of sprue attached to the part or a bit of part still on the sprue. Twisting can also bend or break parts, so you need to cut them free. Some

Ejector-pin marks are unavoidable – they look like this. Take care not to confuse them with marks that should be there like the welded plug mark on the back of this part!

Apply a little filler with your knife tip and press it into the mark. You can practise on ones that won't show after the model is assembled, like the one I'm doing here.

Let it dry, then slice or scrape away the surplus till you see the outline of the original mark with the mark itself full of filler.

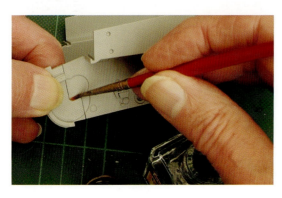

Hold the part in place and run a little liquid cement into the joint with a fine paintbrush. Keep it just for cement, with coloured tape on the handle to identify it.

almost indistinguishable from them, so it is wise to look carefully at both top and bottom to check where to saw.

Small parts will need your knife instead of the saw. Here you need a different technique: hold the part not the sprue! Put the sprue on your cutting mat so that the part is as flat against it as you can manage – turn the sprue over to see which way up is best. Then hold the sprue with at least one finger holding the part as well. Small parts often spring away as they come loose and leave you hunting around your work table and on the floor to find them. Small parts are very light and bounce off whatever they hit, so one may end up a long way from where you thought you saw it fall.

Cutting the part free will leave a small stub of the attachment on it. Use your knife to carefully pare it away, making sure you don't cut into the part itself. You will find that most parts have a tiny plastic

TOP The torsion bars need cement only where I'm pointing; don't get it anywhere else or they won't work.

MIDDLE Note which way the axles point – forward one side, backward on the other.

BOTTOM Here's how the torsion bars fit in the hull.

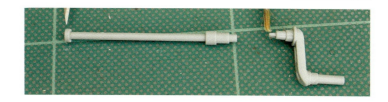

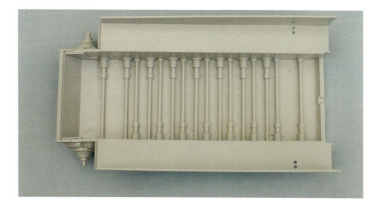

rim around them because the moulds they come from have separate tops and bottoms – some have separate sides as well. This tiny rim is called 'flash' and can be anywhere depending on the part's shape. Scrape it away with your knife blade, working slowly with the blade angled against the part; something around 45 degrees will do for most polystyrene, though its quality varies between kit makers so experiment on an edge of the sprue to see what angle works best. The same cleanup method works for round parts like gun barrels, but for these it's best to scrape diagonally across the flash instead of along it. Try to take the blade around the curve of these parts, to avoid getting a flat place all along the seam. Finish off by very gently filing the same way if scraping still leaves a bit of flash.

Now take another look at the part. Can you see raised or sunken round marks on it? These are 'ejector-pin' marks, used when the sprue was ejected from its mould, and you need to get rid of them – though check that you're not looking at something that's supposed to be there! Raised marks can be sliced away a bit at a time with the tip of your knife blade, scraping gently at the end to get them completely flat. Sometimes they are in a place you cannot reach from the side with your knife, and here you'll find the chisel blade better. Sometime a mark can be raised at one side and sunken at the other, or have a raised rim around a sunken mark, so you may need to slice part of it away and fill the rest.

FILLING SINK MARKS AND JOINTS

Sunken marks will need to be filled with your choice of putty. Take a bit on the tip of your knife blade and press it firmly into the mark, then let it dry. Trying to smooth it while it's damp will make a mess!

You'll have to wait a while, so check by keeping a blob of putty on a bit of paper and poking it occasionally; when you can do this without leaving a fingermark it will be safe to work on your mark. Take a look – has the filler shrunk or does it still stand above the plastic around the mark? If it's shrunk simply add some more and let it dry. If it has not you can pare it down with your knife and finish by scraping it to a smooth flat finish. You can do the same with marks on round objects like the gun barrels I mentioned before, but remember to work diagonally around the barrel and not along it. The same methods are used on 'sink holes' in plastic, where it has shrunk on a particularly thick part after being taken from the mould. Of course, you need not fill anything that will be hidden when the model is built.

Fortunately the first such parts added to this Tiger are G23 and G24, whose marks will be almost completely hidden when the model is finished so you can use them to practise! Use filler in the same way when there is a gap at the joint of assembled parts. And of course you do not need to fill marks on just one part at a time, do a batch and let them dry while you assemble the parts from the last batch.

With the parts cleaned up and ejector-pin marks removed you are ready to put them together. Do they fit properly, without gaps, and

are they straight along their edges? If not, take a careful look to see what stops them fitting properly – it may be a bit of excess plastic that needs to be removed, or a location pin that doesn't fit its hole. When they do fit you can start assembly. Hold the parts together tightly and dip your thin brush for cement into the liquid cement. Touch it to the joint and watch the cement run along it. Dip and touch again where it stopped if you need to complete a long joint. Do this from the inside of as many joints as possible, to avoid getting cement where it shows, and be very sparing with the cement if you must put it on the outside. The result should be a nice clean joint, cemented all along. If softened plastic squeezes out, let it dry and scrape it like flash.

SUSPENSION AND WHEELS

DML provides the option of a movable suspension in this kit, with working torsion bars if you cut off their fixing pins on the hull. This is for modellers who want a scenic base with 'lumps and bumps' on the ground so the wheels need to be articulated to fit them. It is not a 'play feature' to let anyone bounce your model on its suspension! Leave the pins on your hull and have a fixed suspension if you are going to use a flat base or no base at all. If you are going to paint your wheels as separate parts

you can still complete all the other stages of the suspension, but keep the idler axles (parts B26) separate to paint with the wheels because you will need them movable when you fit the tracks.

Follow the assembly sequence in the instructions with some adjustments. The wheels and idler axles, as mentioned, need to be separate until you have painted them and the hull and are ready to fit the tracks. You also need to think about parts that may be easily damaged if fitted too soon. Stage 6 of the instructions, for instance, has you fitting fragile parts to the hull rear before you complete its main structure. Don't do this, but finish the main construction before you add smaller parts. So complete the hull, then the wheels and tracks, and then work on the smaller detail parts. It can be helpful to use a highlighter to mark instructions that you will go back to at a later stage, and then cross them out when each one is dealt with.

MASKING AND PAINTING

For this model I used a Tamiya spray can of German Grey, so I'll talk now about spraying. Before you start look for locating pins, axles and other places where you will need to cement parts together. You don't want paint on those so cut short lengths of masking tape to wrap around the axles where the

More masking tape secures paper over larger areas that need to be shielded from the spray.

The parts of the interior that will be seen through the hatches are ivory with black 'mechanical bits'.

Test your wash where it won't show, on the inside of a centre wheel.

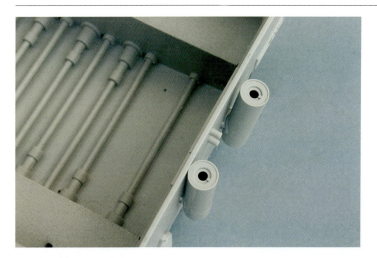

The exhausts lean against the hull if left as DML moulds them; they should be parallel to it.

This is the painted turret. Note the silver area on the gun and the brown case catcher with its black edge.

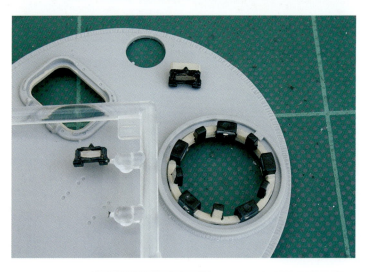

The cupola parts need ivory and black paint like this.

Paint the periscope mirrors silver, and when that's really dry paint the whole body black.

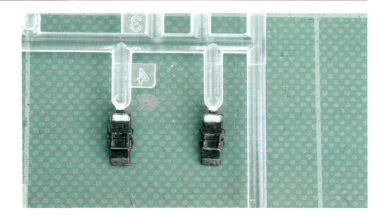

Use a different grey for the tyres. I find it easiest to paint several at a time, in quarters like this, and then turn the sprue to paint the next quarter.

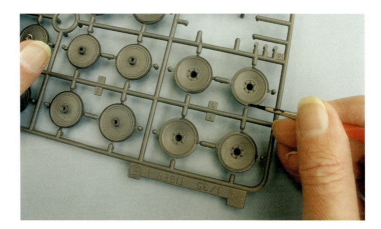

The hull and turret need careful masking including inside their hatches – the turret bottom needs to be masked too.

wheels will fit, and small squares to put over the location points inside and outside each wheel (if you prefer to brush paint you can just take care not to get paint where it should not be). Now put down a thick layer of newspaper – I always spray outside but if you must do it indoors open the windows because the solvents in some paints can make you ill. Now you can lay the hull upside-down in the middle of the paper. Next, find some Blu-Tack or its equivalent – the low-tack putty that's sold to put posters onto walls without marking the paint or wallpaper. Use small blobs of this, or loops of masking tape, to attach each small part to the newspaper around. Spray from the front, then the back, then from each side. Remember, you only need a thin coat of paint – if the plastic colour shows through, just spray again when the first coat is dry. Turn the wheels and axles over when they're dry and spray their other sides.

This kit includes some interior parts for the hull. They are no problem to assemble and fit, but you need to know what colours they should be. The radiator compartment for a Tiger of this vintage was blue-grey, which you can match by mixing Humbrol enamels: 37 parts of No. 34, 10 of No. 25, six of No. 150 and three of No. 80. Yes, that sounds awkward but it isn't really. You need something wide and flat, with a raised lip, to put the paint into –

the top of a yoghurt pot is ideal. Simply dip the spoon end of your Tamiya stirrer into the original paint and count the drops dripping off it into your pot top. Drip into your pot lid as many drops as you need of each enamel, then mix them thoroughly and you have the colour wanted. If you need more paint simply repeat the process. The radiator grilles are metallic grey and their fans are matt aluminium. The fan centres seem to be bronze, and you can paint matt black between the fan blades to indicate empty space under them.

The driver's area has the same blue-grey for its bottom and lower sides, with a creamy colour for the upper sides and front. There is no perfect match for this colour, but I suggest Humbrol No. 71 or No. 103 as reasonably close when seen through an open hatch. The 'mechanical' interior parts of German tanks were almost invariably painted black, but I suggest you use a satin black because matt black is too matt for them.

The instructions tell you to fit the glacis plate, part G19, before the driver's front plate, F20; but F20 has a lip that must fit under G19. Fit the hull sides and roof, then add G19 and finally F20. If you are going to leave your hatches open you will need to fit them and their hinges before fixing the roof. The hatch insides are grey and their hinges and latches are

'mechanical' so need to be black. The co-driver's machine gun has a headpad on a stalk that DML tells you to bend over so it is horizontal. Take your saw and nick the stalk in two or three places on the inside of the intended bend. Now it can bend in tiny segments without breaking, and to keep it in the right shape all you need to do is brush some cement into the nicks and hold until the cement is dry.

Now you can deal with the rest of the painting for the wheels – their tyres and the bare steel left by the tracks rubbing on the sprocket teeth and the rim of the idler wheel. Don't use 'silver' paint for bare steel, as it is much too shiny. Humbrol's polished steel metallic paint is ideal. Paint it on, let it dry, and buff it to a sheen. Be wary of kit instructions for painting tyres, which often tell you to use satin black. Rubber tyres are neither satin nor true black, but a very dark grey. I often use Revell's No. 9 paint for this, but you can also mix your own with matt black and a little white or earth-brown – brown because cross-country tyres often become a brownish dark grey. Now you can add the roadwheels to the model, but leave the sprockets and idlers for later.

ASSEMBLING THE TRACKS

DML provides a former to shape the tracks where they curve around

Make two runs of track for each side.

the sprockets and idlers. The track links come in two bags, and it is important to keep them separate because this version of the Tiger had different links for its two sides. Open just one bag and complete that side before you open the other one. Take a link from your open bag and compare it to the instruction drawings to see which side it goes on, then you can start building. Clean up the links and lay five or six on a flat surface — a glass table-top is ideal, or you could buy a cheap photograph frame and use the glass from that, because you need a surface that the track links will not stick to when you put cement on them. Then press the links together so they meet cleanly and apply a little cement to their joints. Use your metal ruler to make sure they are flat and in a straight line, by first pressing it down onto each side to flatten them and then putting it beside them and pressing them against it. Assemble a few at a time because until you are used to the process it can be hard to keep them straight, flat, and together if you do too many at once; practice will let you assemble more without any problems. Then continue until you have enough links to fit onto the former — the cement will give a

Push a steel ruler against the tracks to keep everything straight.

little so you can shape them round it, though of course you must not wait until it is completely dry. Now you can use the second former for the other end of this track.

When both ends are dry you can fit them to their sprocket and idler and test them on the model without cementing them. They will slip into place quite easily if you line them up with the roadwheels and then align the location holes on the sprocket and idler with their pegs on the hull. Most kits do not yet include those helpful formers, but if you build one of those you will find it easy to curve the tracks around the sprockets and idler instead. Measure the gap between the front and rear of the track and make a note of its length on the tops and bottoms of the wheels, which for most models will be different. Now assemble enough links to fill those gaps. Cement one length to the top of the track that

goes round the sprocket and the other to the bottom of that around the idler, so you finish with two separate sections, and they're ready for painting. Ignore instructions to paint them 'steel', because tank tracks never are bare metal – if new they either have a rust-preventative paint on them or are rusty; if used they will be dirty, not rusty, with bare metal showing on the parts that touch the wheels and ground. Choose a suitable 'earth' colour and paint them with that to show the ground-in dirt on them. Then take whatever 'steel' colour you have chosen and dry-brush along their length. Dry-brushing is a simple process. All you do is dip the tip of your round brush into the paint without getting a lot on it, then wipe its tip against some kitchen paper until it is almost dry. Now you're ready to dry-brush with just enough paint on your brush to give a light coat on the parts of the track that stick up, and that's where the dirt would be worn off. Do the bottoms first, where the ground touches each link, and then turn the track over and dry-brush where the wheels touch them.

Now you can add them to the model. Slip the top section along its wheels from the front and make sure the sprocket is on its peg. Then slip the other section onto the idler, put it and its axle into place, and swing the axle to let the ends meet up. Finally, apply cement to the track ends and the sprocket and idler axles.

This is a good place to mention some points that you'll need to think about on other models. You'll have noticed that I didn't tell you to add the trackguards. This is because they would be in the way when you went to slip the track along the tops of the wheels and cement its ends together. You will need to think about possible obstructions like these while you're getting any model ready for its tracks. Sometimes you can easily add the tracks 'sideways' instead of from front and back, but make sure that you can! You will also find many kits of tanks that used rubber pads on their tracks, the Sherman for instance. You can use the same method to paint those, but you will need to paint the pads after doing the 'steel' dry-brushing. What you will want is some dirt in the rubber, and all that is involved there is to dry-brush your earth colour onto the rubber colour – it won't matter if some gets onto the steel areas because they do get dirty too.

OPTIONAL METAL PARTS

Now you know enough to be able to complete the model using the methods I've shown you if you are only using the plastic parts. But there are some metal parts that are very easy to use, so I'll look at those with you.

First are the front trackguards, where you have the option of three different pairs on the etched-metal fret in the kit as well as the

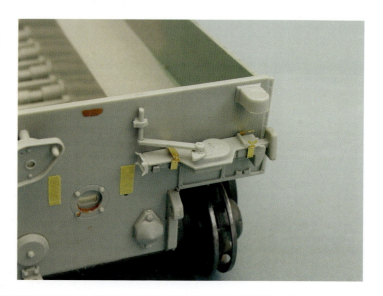

If you use the brass jack securing clasps this is how they fit. I don't recommend using the brass mounts under the jack because they are too thin – the real ones were quite substantial.

Cut brass from its fret by pressing down with a sharp blade, don't drag it across the attachment. Hold the part down with a spare finger so it doesn't get lost – I've kept mine out of the way so you can see the part.

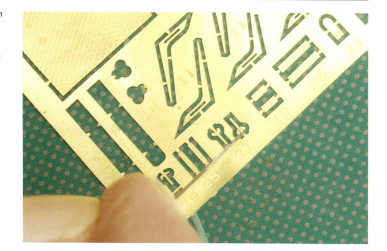

Use tweezers to place the parts in their locating grooves, and apply a drop of superglue with a cocktail stick.

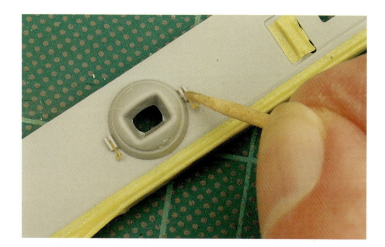

The machine-gunner's headpad is on a stalk that needs to be bent at 90 degrees. To make the bend, saw partway through the stalk in several places inside the bend, then bend gently to shape. Cement will seal the cuts.

Here's the completed machine gun.

Barrels in two halves will have moulding stubs on each half. Cut them down but don't try to clean them right off yet. Hold the halves together and apply cement all along its length. Wait till the cement is fully dry and then gently scrape the seam off. Then cut the moulding stubs away very slowly and carefully to keep the barrel round and scrape across it to finish removing the stubs. You can do this with a fine file if you prefer.

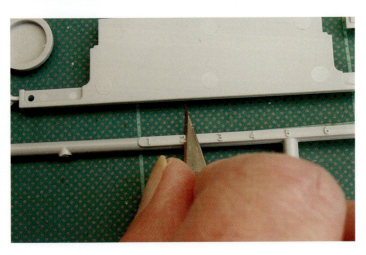

DML gives you casting numbers to add to the top of the gun mantlet. Slice them off the sprue with your blade edge flat against it.

The gun barrel's retainer doesn't fit like this inside the breech as the instructions show, but the other way up.

Three kinds of tow shackles are provided. Use the one in the centre of the photograph, which is correct for this tank and needs no clean up.

There are location points for several different turret stowage bin arrangements, showing as raised lines. Gently scrape away the ones for the bins you don't use.

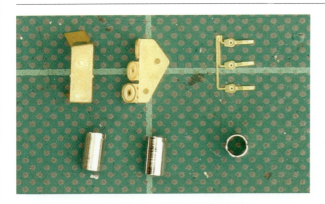

The metal parts for the smoke mortars are tricky to use but worth it if you are already used to tiny metal bits. The plastic ones are not quite as detailed but are very easy to use.

The rear view shows the shape of the wiring harness, which is tricky to bend and not really noticeable as missing if you use the plastic version.

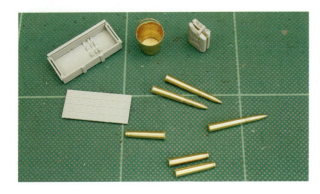

DML provides accessories including turned brass shells, empty shell cases, ammo boxes, jerrycans and a bucket for you to use as you like.

moulded plastic ones. Choose the one you like and cut it free with your knife blade; the metal is thin enough that you won't have a problem if you hold it flat on your cutting mat and press down with the blade. You will be left with a little stub of metal where you cut it. Hold it with your smooth-jawed pliers, with the stub sticking out, and file along the part, not across it, until the stub has gone. If the part bends you can straighten it by squeezing it flat again with the pliers. There's no bending line on the back of each trackguard, but you can easily make your own. Measure on the plastic version to see where the bend should be, then measure the same distance on the metal part and score gently two or three times across its back. That will be quite enough to let you bend it without getting a curve instead of an angle. To attach it you need superglue. Put a tiny drop on the end of a wooden cocktail stick or toothpick and place it on the plastic part. Quickly place the metal guard onto it, making sure

Painting tools and exhausts

I haven't mentioned the colours of the tools yet. Choose a pale wood colour for their handles, but the metal heads should be satin black and the clasps moulded onto them are grey like the rest of the tank. The wire cutters, part K10, also have black metal parts but their handles are a red-brown. Use your fine brush to paint parts like these, and work slowly to avoid getting the wrong colours on the grey camouflage.

Let's think about the exhaust pipes now. These were ordinary thin steel and got rusty quite quickly because of water vapour in the hot exhaust fumes. They were nearly always painted, either black or the main camouflage colour, before a tank left the factory but the heat tended to burn the paint off them. This gives you several options for the exhausts on a model tank – either painted with a bit of rust at their open ends, or rusty all over. There are several ways to give the rusty appearance, and the one I used here was to give them a base coat of red-brown paint. The next step is to use watercolours from an artists' shop to give their rusty appearance. Burnt sienna, burnt umber and light red will let you produce the right effects and you can mix them to vary the shades. Dip your cheap brush into water and pick up a little of the lightest colour on it. Take some off on kitchen paper as if you were going to dry-brush, and then stipple it onto the exhaust. (Stippling is dabbing the brush lightly up and down on the part and will spoil a good brush.) Now do the same with the middle colour, and then with the dark one. What you should have now is a varied, mottled finish where the three watercolours have merged. If it looks too even, just repeat the process with more of the colours till it looks right.

TOP TO BOTTOM

Painting exhausts stage 1. Here I've added a first mottle of dark rust-brown watercolour over the base coat of red-brown.

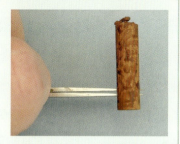

Painting exhausts stage 2. Next comes a mottle of mid-rust.

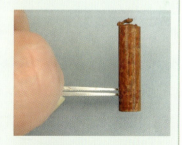

Painting exhausts stage 3. Finally a mottle of light rust completes the job. The watercolour dries matt but is still wet in these photos.

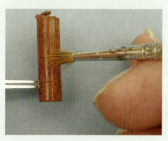

Stipple the rust tones on like this with a cheap brush.

that you have it straight, and press down. If it slips out of alignment you can remove it by slipping your knife blade carefully under it to pop it off, and try again.

The second metal part you might like to use is the gun barrel. It's a nice turned aluminium barrel that has no seam to be removed. The plastic and metal barrels can be made to 'move back to firing position after recoiling' with the spring included in the kit, and you should fit the spring to keep the barrel extended to the right length. The metal barrel is very

Paint the machine-gun barrels black after spraying the grey on the tank, and metallize them with the edge of a pencil.

easy to use: just trap its spring between the breech parts as shown by the instructions and use another drop of superglue to attach the muzzle brake.

Most of the turret interior parts need painting before fitting to the turret. They are all that creamy colour, but with areas of other colours. The seats have satin black seat and backrest cushions, and you should make sure to attach the loader's seat (A5 and A8) facing the back of the turret – the instruction sheet in my kit has it the wrong way, facing forward, but might have been revised when you buy yours. The gun breech assembly is all cream except for the polished steel of the insides of parts A5 and A6 and the brown canvas of the empty shellcase catcher, A22. The commander's cupola has clear vision blocks and their surrounds and cushions should be satin black.

Applying the decals

The next step is to add the decals for your chosen subject, with several alternatives depending on which optional parts you chose to use. The Tamiya spray provides an ideal surface, just glossy enough to avoid a 'silvering' effect without being too glossy to look correct on the model. 'Silvering' is the term used to describe the silvery look of the clear areas of any decal when it is put onto a matt-painted surface, and is caused by air trapped in the rough surface of matt paint.

Cut round your chosen decals with scissors or a knife, it doesn't matter which, but try not to cut into their clear surrounds because good decals have it tapered down to their edges so there's no obvious edge on the model. Float each decal on water and watch for it to start coming loose. Use your tweezers to pick it out of the water and place it on the model, then slide the decal off its paper to the right place. Check that it is straight and level, then gently press it down with a soft cloth – an old handkerchief is ideal. Blot away any water that squeezes out from under

RIGHT Here's the Tiger with all parts fitted and painted and decals applied, but before a final wash to weather the sides and top.

it, and then let it dry without touching it.

Now you have a completed Tiger, so all that's left is a bit of 'weathering' – making it look dirty as if it had been rolling across fields. You can have a lot of fun with this process once you get used to it, in fact the only problem will be deciding when to stop! This time I will just make it look dusty with a 'wash', a very dilute coat of paint the same earth colour that I used on the tracks. Put some paint into your yoghurt pot top and add enough thinner to make it almost transparent. Dip your largest brush into this and rest it against a wheel, letting the wash run off the brush by itself. You want it in the recess at the centre of the wheel and running around its rim onto the tyre. Repeat with a bit more paint in the wash if it seems too transparent, but remember that you're aiming for a dirty effect, not a tank covered in mud. Don't forget to get your wash behind the wheels as well, all over the lower hull sides and under the bottoms of the sponsons and trackguards. My model is meant to look fairly clean, without more than the dirt on its lower hull and a little on the hull front and rear, so I only used the wash on those surfaces that would collect thick dust. That means the tops of the front trackguards and the glacis between them, the driver's front plate with his visor and the lower parts of the hull rear. As a rule you should avoid making vertical surfaces too dirty: dust tends to fall off them on a real tank unless there's a great deal of it, but if your model is supposed to be going across dry, dusty ground it will collect a lot more and the sides and top surfaces will be dirty too. Remember, trackguards are there to stop dust spraying up all over the place so only a tank that's not been cleaned for a long time will be really mucky if all it has to worry about is dust. Mud, on the other hand, will stick wherever it lands.

The overall grey finish is broken up by red primer inside the radiator hatch and green smoke bombs.

MORE PAINTING AND FINISHING IDEAS AND SIMPLE IMPROVEMENTS

Of course there are other ways to paint and weather your models. Here are some ideas, together with hints about painting crew figures.

HINTS ABOUT BRUSH PAINTING

I'm sure I don't need to tell anyone how to use a paintbrush, but here are some tips. First, stir the paint thoroughly for at least a minute until there are no more lumps or thicker parts that resist your stirrer, and be sure to go around the edges of the tin, not just in the middle of the paint. Stir it several times during any long painting session, to make sure the pigment doesn't start to separate from its clear carrier.

Second, keep your brush clean not just at the end of painting but while you are painting. Dip it in thinners and wipe it off on kitchen paper whenever paint starts building up on it – this makes painting easier.

Third, watch for thick paint – some makes do tend to go thicker in their pots while you are painting. If the paint starts getting thick and difficult to brush evenly onto your model, put a little thinner into the pot and stir thoroughly.

Finally, think about the directions that the brush should

move in. On vertical surfaces like hull and turret sides you should brush up and down so that any marks you leave look like normal variations in the colour under the dust. On horizontal surfaces like the hull top you should brush along the model, but if there's a sideways slope anywhere you should brush toward the side for the same effect. If you see that you will need more than one coat of paint to get an even finish, brush along the sides and across the top so that any brush marks are evened out with the final coat.

HOW TO DO A 'SPRAYED' FINISH WITHOUT AN AIRBRUSH

How do you get a sprayed, soft-edged division between colours without an airbrush? Here's how I do it. Begin by painting the basic colour over the whole model as far as your earth colour, and dry-brush more down over the edges of the earth. Now take a cheap size 3 brush. Don't use the one you already have, it

will be no good for much else when you've done the next step – which is to cut most of its bristles down to 2mm or a bit less to leave a short stub. Dip it stub into the second colour paint and wipe it on kitchen paper as if you were about to dry-brush.

Now stipple the paint around the outline of the first area you want that colour. Stay a little inside the outline needed, then you can move outward a little if the first outline is too 'solid'. You should have a soft edge around the second colour when you have done it correctly, with the first showing through it where they merge. Then stipple more second colour a bit more heavily over the inner edge of your outline and then more heavily still up over the new inner edge. The result should graduate from very thin cover at the outside to quite solid on the inside. Now pick up a normal brush and fill in the rest of the area. Clean your stippling brush between areas so the paint does not build up on it. When done, you will have the nearest match to a blurred-edge

Make your own headlamp reflectors

Here's a simple way to make your own reflectors. Take a small square of kitchen foil, shiny side up, and gently burnish it into the lamp body with the rounded end of a brush. Don't worry about tiny creases or splits, they won't show behind the lens. Now put the foil shiny side down on your cutting mat and cut round the edge of your new reflector. The result is a shiny reflector that fits neatly inside the lamp and can be popped into place after you have painted your model. The lens itself will be spoilt, though, if you use plastic cement or superglue to attach it – they usually make it foggy inside. Use white glue instead, it will dry clear and will not fog the lens. When you weather your model don't forget to add dust to the nice shiny lenses as well.

LEFT TO RIGHT

You need a square of kitchen foil for the reflector. It's easier to hold the lamp if you leave it on the sprue till you've finished modifying it.

Place the foil shiny side up and burnish it gently into the lamp with the rounded end of a suitably sized paintbrush.

Burnish the foil all round the edge too, to give a cutting mark. Creases or small splits won't show behind the lens.

Turn the foil over and cut around the edge of the reflector, pressing down with the blade not slicing along it.

You now have a reflector that fits neatly inside the lamp and below its lens location ridge.

Use white glue, or a clear parts glue, to fix the foil reflector into the map body and the lens over it and you get this realistic result.

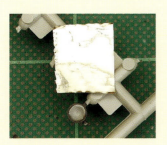

PAINTING WINTER WHITEWASH

There are many ways of painting winter white, and some of them are very artistic. Many modellers use an airbrush to paint thin white patches over a base colour. My personal method just copies the original method.

You need a small tube of students' white watercolour paint. Fold a piece of kitchen paper into four to make a pad and squeeze some paint onto it. Dip your size 3 brush into the paint and smear it onto the model. Keep on till you complete the pattern as you want it, and don't be afraid to go over parts of it with extra paint if it looks too thin – decide for yourself how thick or thin the white coverage was. Let it dry while you think about where it would wear away from the crew walking on it and opening hatches, or from brushing against bushes while going across country. When you've decided your 'wear pattern', bend a pipe-cleaner in two so its wire won't scratch your paint where you don't want it scratched. Now just rub it on the white and you'll find it works exactly like the wear imposed by boots, hands or bushes. Add some horizontal scratches along the sides for more 'wear by bushes' if you want.

You'll see on my model that paint is worn on the top of the gun barrel too. That's because this was a convenient place for the crew to grab while climbing on board. This is a different kind of wear, but

just as easy to reproduce. All I did was to dip a small brush into water and place it against the white watercolour. The water dissolves the colour and leaves a lovely blurred edge to the worn patch, and you can do the same on other areas. I have added an extra touch to the wooden tool handles for this model by using Citadel's ready-made 'flesh wash' on them. This gives them the varnished appearance of tools seen in colour photographs of German tanks.

TOP TO BOTTOM

The best way to reproduce whitewash is white watercolour paint.

Hold the model at an angle so you can paint it with strokes where you could reach if you were 2in. tall.

When the watercolour is dry, rub it where you want it worn away. Use a doubled-over pipe-cleaner to avoid scratches, but of course add scratches deliberately where you think they might have occurred. Perhaps along the side when the tank drove between thorny bushes?

sprayed finish that is possible without using an airbrush.

DAMAGING RUBBER TYRES

Real tanks often have chunks missing from their tyres or rubber track pads, due to collecting stones and debris on their tracks which chip bits off the rubber. It's easy to reproduce this, just take your file and run it across the edge of the tyre in a few places.

ANOTHER WAY OF PAINTING EXHAUST PIPES

Here's a different technique for exhausts. The same red-brown base coat is used but this time the rust effect is made with pastel pigments. These are specially-formulated coloured 'dusts' and there are several makes available. They come in a wide range of rust, dirt, earth, sand and dust colours, and I use those made by MIG Productions. You use them by dipping a brush into the pot and stroking or stippling it where you want the pigment.

THINNING TRACKGUARD ENDS

Most kits have trackguard ends moulded fairly thick so you need to thin down an exposed end to look more like the thin metal of the real thing. Use a sharp knife blade to carve away the underside. Then nick upwards a little bit in from

each side, and finally carve the underside to meet your nicks. What you are aiming for is a bevelled edge that disappears under the trackguard. This method can be used anywhere that you need to show the end of a thin metal part.

ADDING HIGHLIGHTS

Adding highlights is a simple job but you do need to decide where to put them. First mix a little white into the base colour paint, just enough to lighten it slightly. Then look at the model and identify all its corners, like where the hull top meets the sides. Dry-brush a little of your lightened colour across them. Then look for raised features like hatch hinges, and dry-brush those too. Now add a little more white to your mix and repeat the process, but dry-brushing much more lightly. You can do this as many times as you like – some modellers even end up with pure white for the greatest highlights, but be careful because the result can look exaggerated.

The nice thing about this dry-brushing of highlights is that if you decide it looks wrong you can simply go back over your highlights with the original paint and start again.

A further idea is to paint the more or less horizontal surfaces, the hull and turret tops and sloping glacis, with a slightly lightened paint in the first place.

This helps to reproduce the effect of natural light falling on a tank from above. Some modellers also like to use a darkened wash in recesses and around such things as raised rivet- or bolt-heads, just to emphasize them a bit more. You can try all these ideas out for yourself and see which you like. Practise until you have the results you want!

APPLYING DECALS OVER MATT PAINT

Matt paint under a decal is likely to produce the 'silvering' that I mentioned before, because its rough surface traps air under the decal. To avoid this, produce a smooth surface by brushing gloss varnish over the matt paint. Unfortunately most varnishes tend to alter the colour under them a little, so you need to cover all of your model that isn't already weathered with an earth colour, and then add the decals.

To help the decals lie down over raised details, and sink into recesses, you will find 'decal setting solution' from several different manufacturers. Some are intended to go under the decal, painted onto the model, and others go over the decal when it's in place, but both types soften its transparent carrier film. All you do when using them is press the decal gently over the details. Let it dry a while and look closely – if it has not laid over the details cleanly just add more

To highlight metal details, Humbrol silver and steel coloured enamels were toned down with raw umber oil paint and dry-brushed onto the surface of the model, in this case the engine of a StuG III.

To highlight the metal part of the tracks that touch the ground and running gear, Humbrol's enamel silver and steel were dry-brushed onto the raised surfaces.

solution and press down again till you're satisfied. Test the solution you've bought before using it, by applying it to a decal you won't be using on the model so you can check that it does not react in any way with the ink — some solutions are stronger than others, and some decals are weaker than others. If the test decal's ink starts to run or its clear backing film disintegrates all you have to do is dilute the solution with a little water and make another test. Problems are rare, but the test is so simple that it's always worth doing.

When all the decals are satisfactorily placed and dry, paint matt varnish over the whole model to cover up the gloss finish. Brush it like the paint, along the top surfaces and down the sides so that any streaks look like rain and dust marks.

Using rubdown decals

There's an alternative to the waterslide decals that come in kits: rubdown or 'dryprint' decals, made by Archer Fine Transfers and other companies. The images are printed on the back of a special translucent sheet, backed by paper, and to release one you just rub across the top of the sheet until it comes away and settles where you want it, then press carefully to make sure it is firmly attached. To avoid rubbing down adjacent decals you need to cut the one you want free from the backing sheet with the tip of your knife blade (scissors tend to make adjacent decals pop off the sheet). Cut with enough space around it to pick it up with your tweezers! Then position it on the model and rub the back of its backing sheet with a soft, rounded pencil or ballpoint pen.

Base coat or undercoat?

These two terms mean much the same thing, because as I mentioned in building the first Tiger model two or three thin coats are much better than one thick one. This applies whether you use a spray can, a brush or an airbrush. Some modellers use a base coat different to the camouflage colour, often in light grey, to both show up any faults in joints that need to be filled and give a common base finish to any metal, resin or other different materials combined with the plastic of a kit. Others like to use black for a base coat, adding the camouflage over it more thinly at the edges of panels so that the black shows through the colour

TOP To apply waterslide decals, the surface of the model was coated with acrylic gloss in the necessary area.

MIDDLE To allow the decals to soften and conform to the surface and set without showing trapped air (silvering) Solvaset solution was applied to both over and under the marking.

BOTTOM After the decals had dried, they were sealed with a flat lacquer finish, which helps to hide the edge of the carrier film.

and darkens it to give a 'shadow' effect. I don't do this because I have spent many years looking at real tanks and never seen darker paint in corners. What collects there is dirt, so should be shown as dirt. My own preference is to use the base camouflage colour as an undercoat. It does exactly the same job as any other colour in showing up faults to be dealt with and unifying the surfaces of metal, resin and plastic but saves one coat of paint – and although several thin coats are better than one thick one I still don't want to hide the details on a model by adding yet another one as an undercoat!

Stencils

Instead of decals, whether waterslide or rubdown, you can use stencils to put the markings onto your models. Some are made in thin metal and some in masking film. Either type can be found in some etched sets, and you can also buy stencils separately from some makers. They do have the advantage of producing the exact appearance of a painted marking with no film around it, but need care in use. In the first place you must make sure to have them pressed very tightly to the model surface, either by holding metal ones down with masking tape or by pressing the self-adhesive ones into place very firmly. This is critically important, because any gaps around the image will let your paint bleed under its edge and spoil the marking. I don't recommend that you try to use stencils with spraycans, because these cover too wide an area so you would need to mask off most of the model around the stencil. Airbrush users can adjust the amount of paint delivered to avoid that problem. Alternatively, use the

The model has been primer coated with a dark brown lacquer paint, which provides a foundation for the base colour.

Tamiya's acrylic German Dark Yellow was sprayed onto the dark brown surface, allowing the primer to show through as a pre-shade to the finished coat.

'stippling brush' that I've described to stipple the paint over the stencil image in several thin coats so the paint is a solid colour. Remove the stencil carefully when the paint is almost dry, not completely dry in case you drag some paint off the marking. If any 'bleeding' has happened you can touch in the edge with a fine brush and the camouflage colour.

SCALE COLOUR

'Scale colour' is a term used to describe lightening a camouflage colour to reproduce the effect of looking at a tank some distance away – you can see this effect by scanning from right in front of you to the distance anywhere. The green grass, or the brick buildings, will seem to be different colours at different distances. All you have to do is add a little white or very pale grey to the colour. But this technique leaves your model looking as though you were seeing it 100 yards away – at which distance you could not see details like rivets and even some larger fittings would be hard to pick out, so why spend time modelling them? In actual fact you are looking at a small replica of the tank, with all its details reduced in size but nevertheless visible, so its colours should be as you see them nearby. The best aircraft, car and ship modellers do not seem to believe in 'scale colour' and I recommend that you avoid this technique. On the other hand, it can be helpful to lighten the paint if the camouflage colour is very dark, because too dark a colour can hide those nice details! You will often see that old photographs seem to show quite a pale colour on tanks that were actually painted dark green, olive drab or German grey. This is simply because they are covered in dust, or have paint that has faded in very bright sunlight. Use the wash technique to add a dusty appearance to the

Instead of using decals, stencils can be used for painting markings on armour models. This is an example of a brass product from Stencilit of Scotland.

whole model, most heavily on horizontal surfaces, and make your camouflage paler if you are copying a photograph of a faded tank – but check the photograph carefully! If you can see a dark colour in places like the top of its gun barrel, or where the crew's hands rest, you are seeing the true paint and the lighter areas are dust that you should try to reproduce. Remember that the service life of most tanks was quite short due to enemy action, so their paint did not have time to fade.

CHIPS AND SCRATCHES

Adding chip marks and scratches to a model is very easy. Just use a fine brush and paint them on where you think paint might have been chipped or worn away from the real tank, or the paint scratched by pushing through heavy undergrowth or by knocking down brick walls. However, be careful not to overdo it! This technique became popular after the First Gulf War because almost all the captured Iraqi tanks had very badly worn and chipped paint. What is often overlooked is that those tanks had been badly painted in the first place, with poor-quality paint added over their original factory finishes so it's not surprising that it wore very quickly to show the original paint underneath. Most of the tanks you model will have been properly painted, with paint that did not chip off or wear away easily. Any chips and wear that did occur would be likely to show dark brown armour steel, not bright silver like the results of a modern car crash unless they were on 'ordinary' steel parts such as trackguards or are on a modern aluminium-armoured vehicle like the M113 series. If you are showing chips in a temporary finish such as winter whitewash they will show the original camouflage underneath it, of course.

THE BASICS OF CREW FIGURES AND BYSTANDERS

Now that we've dealt with the tanks it's time to think about figures to go with them, both those in the kits and the ones you can buy separately. Plastic ones come in either normal hard plastic or DML's special plastic, like the figures in the Tiger kit. You can also buy a wide range of white-metal and resin figures, and sometimes you can make a more individual figure by switching the arms, legs or heads that come in a kit, but you can also buy sets of heads and even hands from several makers to let you personalize them even more.

Assembly is the same for all of them, but read the chapters that deal with white metal and resin for tips on handling these materials before you tackle figures made of them. Clean the parts up as usual,

To simulate the effect of worn or chipped paint, a darker pigment of lacquer was applied with a fine 000 brush.

Applied to areas of typical wear and tear like around crew hatches and other access points, the paint chipping effect can easily be overdone.

Altering a head – Denis Allaire

FROM TOP LEFT

The figure is one of the German tanker offerings by TANK in 1/35-scale resin. Denis Allaire will alter the head for one of the aftermarket Hornet offerings.

Denis uses very sharp pliers to snip off the moulded-on head. It is crucial to place the blades well above the collar and to ensure that the blades cut parallel to the collar.

The head has been removed and the neck has been sanded down lightly.

With a drilling tool, Denis then drills out the neck area being very careful not to allow the drill bit to run too closely to the collar. The best approach is to start by drilling a hole directly in the centre of the neck and enlarging the hole by rotating the drill tool in a pivoting motion.

The neck has been drilled out and is ready to accommodate a new head.

The new head placed on the figure.

Finished figure.

The line of watercolours from Vallejo are ideal for detail and figure painting. Their dense pigment allows excellent coverage, and the paint flows very smoothly from a fine brush. This works out well for painting the piping on German uniforms, for example.

but be careful not to cut off things that stick out, like ears, and to look carefully at creases and undercuts so you don't miss any mould parting lines in them. You don't need to clean the parting lines off parts that are going to be hidden inside a turret! You may find an extra tool useful here, Mission Models' Micro Chisel, which has a very narrow chisel tip for getting into small spaces and also a curved one that can make it much easier to work inside rounded folds and creases.

Dry-fit the parts and check that all the joints meet properly. You may need to file or trim these areas, or to use filler to build up a joint. Check also that you will be able to reach all areas with your paintbrush — it may be easier to paint some parts separately, adding them later and touching up the paint at the joint. If you are modifying a kit figure to a different pose take a look at yourself in a mirror to check the pose — for example, a raised arm means that the shoulder goes up too, so you may need to build it up with putty. This also lets you check how the clothing will crease in a different pose. If you don't have a full-length mirror ask a friend to take the pose for you to see.

Painting

Put a thin coat of matt white paint on all exposed flesh — usually just the face and hands. It doesn't matter if this goes onto non-flesh areas, but flesh will always need it. Next is a coat of 'flesh colour' on the same places. Different makers' 'flesh' comes in slightly different tones but none of them looks much like European skin at this stage and most tank crew figures are Northern European types. Highlight and shade this with lighter and darker tones of flesh — take another look in the mirror to see where they should be. Next, use your finest brush to put dots of black on the eyeballs — at any distance only the black pupils are visible. Make sure both eyes point in the same direction, and if your man has his head turned his eyes should be looking further in the direction of the turn. You can add a very little red to your flesh colour to paint lips, but do avoid a 'lipstick' effect.

It's easier to paint clothing from the skin out, so shirt and tie are next. Kit makers don't always suggest the right colours, but the books, magazines and websites I mention in the 'References' chapter will help you with uniforms. Use your 000 brush to highlight them with a little white mixed into the colours you use. Now you can move on to the jacket and trousers. Use a base colour with shadows and highlights as you did for the skin, and vary this a bit by using a slightly different base for the jacket and trousers and for figures that will be near each other — uniforms weren't all made from the same batch of cloth so weren't the same colour all over. For German tank crews you need black uniforms, but there are shades of black just like any other colour. Pure flat black is the colour of the deepest creases and shadows on a cloth garment, but the rest of it looks lighter — not grey but not quite black either.

Painting a figure – Mark Bannerman

FROM TOP LEFT

A 1/35-scale Hornet Italian tanker uniform painted in enamels. The trousers were painted in Humbrol Slate Grey and the jacket was first painted in Dark Earth with several filters of Matt Black mixed with 90 per cent Testors' thinners .

The head was primed in white primer, and then base-painted in Tamiya Desert Yellow mixed 50:50 with Tamiya Matt White. Once the base had dried, I applied a wash of raw umber oil paints and allowed it to fill in all shadow areas.

The flesh tone colour was applied very thinly using a mix of titanium white, gold ochre and burnt sienna oil paints in a 3:1:1 mix. I then added more white to the mix and stippled the highlight colour onto the bridge of

(continued on page 45)

Painting a figure — continued

the nose, upper cheeks and forehead. Note the dark eyes as a result of the raw umber wash in the previous step. The beard was painted using Humbrol Dark Brown and washed in black oil paints.

The cheeks were shadowed using a very small amount of burnt sienna mixed with the original oil flesh base colour. Highlights were added using pure titanium white on the upper cheeks, nose bridge and forehead.

The helmet was stained with burnt sienna.

The eyes were painted using toothpick splinters and a mix of an off-white oil colour. Once the whites of the eyes were dry, raw umber was used for the irises. A highlight of Humbrol 93 was also applied to the beard. The helmet was painted with a thin layer of raw umber over a completely dry burnt sienna base.

ABOVE The figure placed on a scenic diorama with an Italian M14/41 (tank and diorama by Arthur Sekula).

For these, use black with a little grey mixed into it as the base colour and pure black for the shadows. Add a little more grey for the highlight areas. Paint in small sections with the second colour ready-mixed so you can put it on before the first dries. Wet paint will tend to blend where the two colours meet, and you can gently stroke the second colour into the base as well.

Details like badges, buttons and belt buckles are tiny, so you'll need a steady hand and fine brush to paint them. A magnifying glass on a stand will be very useful, and if it has a built-in light that will make painting even easier. The alternative is the 'Optivisor' type of magnifier, basically a headband with magnifying glasses attached to it, which is what I use. The simplest solution, though, is a cheap pair of reading glasses. They come in a selection of strengths so choose whichever feels comfortable for very close work.

As an alternative to painting badges you can use special rubdown decals made by Archer Fine transfers. They're used in the same way as for tank markings, but you may need to cut bits away so they fit properly. Shoulderboards, for instance, must look as if they're coming out from under the collar. Archer also makes 'Ez-Eyes', tiny coloured discs that reproduce human eyes without needing paint.

Painting a head – Mark Bannerman

FROM TOP LEFT

A 1/35-scale Hornet resin head.

The head primed in two light coats of white Tamiya Primer.

A light application of 61 Humbrol Flesh mixed with 20 per cent 34 White.

A light wash of Winsor and Newton Raw Umber oil paint mixed with 20 per cent Testors' thinners.

A first application of Flesh using a mix of Winsor and Newton Burnt Sienna, Titanium White and Gold Ochre in a 1:3:1 mix. A first highlight of the same mix using more Titanium White was added to the upper cheeks, forehead and the bridge of the nose.

The cheeks and lower lip stained with the flesh oil mix with a touch of Humbrol 73 Matt Wine added in. More highlights were added using pure Titanium White. The side cap base-painted in a mix of 70 per cent Humbrol 33 Matt Black mixed with 61 Flesh.

The eyes and teeth filled in using toothpick splinters. A very light beard growth applied using Payne's Grey oil paint mixed with the flesh oil mix. The hair painted using Humbrol 29 Matt Dark Earth then washed in raw umber oil paints. A very fine application of Dark Earth mixed with 33 White added for eyebrows but kept subtle to suggest a fair-haired figure The last step is a few light applications of Glosscoat to bring out a slight sheen in the face.

Highlight and shade – Brian Wildfong

FROM TOP LEFT

Brian Wildfong demonstrates adding highlights and shadows to a 1/35-scale Tamiya figure from the Wespe Crew set. The figure has been assembled and given a coat of primer (Krylon brand aerosol).

The figure is first base-coated with acrylic colours. Some of the sculpted detail on the greatcoat can be seen, but the overall impression is too monotone and flat. Adding shadows and highlights with oils will emphasize the folds, seams and other moulded details.

The deep shadows are blocked in. A darker field grey, mixed from Winsor and Newton Ivory Black, Gold Ochre, Titanium White and French Ultramarine oil paint, has been laid into the deep folds and seams, and around details like shoulder straps and buttons.

Next, highlights are blocked in. Here, a lighter version of the base colour has been mixed by adding some Winsor and Newton Gold Ochre and Titanium White to Ivory Black. This light olive colour is laid in next to the shadow areas.

The entire coat now has a thin layer of either the highlight or shadow colour in oils. The boundary between highlight and shadow is too harsh, however, and will need to be softened by lightly jabbing and stabbing the borders with a dry brush, blending the oils together along their edges.

Winsor and Newton Ivory Black has been blended to darken the colour of a few of the deepest folds and has also been used to outline buttons, seams, pockets, shoulder straps and belt. A lighter version of the highlight colour has been applied to the edges of cuffs, collar, shoulder straps and pockets, and has also been applied to the tops of a few of the wrinkles, especially on the sleeves. Compared to the base-coated figure we started with, the flat-looking greatcoat colour now displays much more depth, detail and variety.

RIGHT The finished figure. A coat of Dullcote was applied to the entire figure to eliminate the glossy finish.

THE BASICS OF BASES

You do not have to put your finished model on a base, though if you want to put any figures beside your tank some kind of base is essential. But one is not needed if all you have is the tank itself and limited space to display it.

Having said that, what kinds of base can you get? The first, and simplest, is a shaped piece of wood. You can get these from many places, and in various sizes. They range from polished mahogany with a carved border to a simple plinth in 'ordinary' wood. You can also just buy a plain piece of wood from a timber merchant's offcut bin and varnish it yourself.

The next simplest bases are commercial ones. These come in many varieties, sizes and prices from many makers. They can be cast in resin or ceramic (plaster), or moulded from expanded polystyrene with a hard skin. They range from simple 'countryside' scenes, to which you add your own grass and other scenery, to complete kits with streets and buildings.

The more complicated bases are those made from scratch. The bottom layer can be a wood or chipboard base with your own addition of 'groundwork' (a very literal term meaning you build up a landscape from the bare earth) on top of it. I won't go here into the methods for constructing one like that, instead I'll concentrate on the 'kit' type.

A SIMPLE COUNTRYSIDE BASE

This one is a straightforward base in moulded expanded polystyrene with a hard skin. It comes with simple groundwork moulded onto it, in this case hollows and rises, a ditch, a few stones, some logs and some tank tracks, but you have to add grass or other vegetation yourself. Mine had some holes where the cooling resin produced bubbles that broke the surface, but these were easily fixed with model filler. You could paint this as desert sand and stones, but the desert doesn't have trees so you'd need to cut away the logs for that. I made mine with vegetation typical of uncultivated land in north-west Europe.

The first step is to paint the basic colours on the ground surface. This is best done with

This is what the base looks like if you simply paint it in shades of green. Not very realistic!

TOP LEFT Here I've painted the logs and picked out some bare earth areas.

MIDDLE LEFT Now some bushes and tufts of grass have been added. It looks better already.

BOTTOM LEFT The white glue dries clear so won't show later.

enamels, which have a longer drying time than acrylic paints and let you use a 'wet on wet' technique. This means putting one colour on a small part of the base and then adding another to it immediately so the two blend together at their meeting point, then painting the next small section and so on. Here you need several earth browns, a medium tone for the base coat with a darker one for the hollows and a paler one on the high points. You can paint the logs as old, weathered grey wood.

The addition of some grass and bushes will make it look much more interesting. Woodland Scenics, available from any good model railway shop, have a range of different-coloured grasses sold in packs of strands about 70mm long, which you cut to whatever length you want for your grass. Several makers offer 'grass mats', which are mats of short grass-like leaves bonded onto a brown paper backing. Those are fine if you want to only have short grass and all the same colour. To get the variation that is seen in real grass you need to find several grass mats in different colours, cut irregular

TOP Hold the 'tree' with tweezers to put it in the hole with a little glue.

BOTTOM The Woodland Scenics foliage and glue that I used.

shapes from them to stick onto your base, and vary the height of the grass they provide by cutting some of it shorter with scissors.

Woodland Scenics' Fine-Leaf Foliage is a dried natural product that gives a very realistic effect of leaves on branches. They have several colours of this, and all you need to do is pull pieces apart to suit the effect you want. Although intended for OO and HO scale railways it works very well as small bushes and short, young tree saplings. Their Underbrush Clump-Foliage, also available in several colours, is very useful to make small, densely leaved plant clumps. All can be glued in place with Woodland Scenics' Scenic Glue, which dries to a clear matt finish. Since it dries matt it won't help if you want puddles of rainwater on your base, for which you need their Water Effects, a special heavier version of white glue that dries glossy and can even be built up in layers to make small streams.

Add this vegetation to your base by making holes with a drill bit – your fingers can push a bit through the surface hardening of this kind of base, but you'll need to use your pin vice or minidrill for resin or ceramic bases. These will take the bottoms of your saplings, and more holes can take some 'long grass' representing the tall weeds that appear in places on uncultivated ground. The Clump-Foliage will make dense low growth here and there.

So far so good, but the effect is still of a painted base with some foliage added to it. Silflor makes some excellent Grass Tufts as well as a different grass mat. This is not on a paper backing sheet so can be pulled into whatever shape you

Here's the finished base with Silflor added and a tank in place on it.

A view into the ditch shows the lusher growth in its bottom where there's more water for the plants, and at its edges where animals and people don't tread down the leaves.

want and stuck down on a base painted in earth colours to look as real as the grass in your garden with the earth showing through it. The double-thickness type makes a quite convincing layer of heather-type growth.

Place all these randomly, leaving bare paths between them where animals and people might walk, and add tufts and long grass by the logs and the low growth, too. My base was laid out to reproduce the general look of real uncultivated land near my home in Sussex, which it has done quite successfully. The final job is to paint a gloss black edge round the base.

Remember that the bottoms of ditches, like the banks of streams, are damper than the higher ground so tend to have lusher, longer vegetation with brighter foliage. Long grass and tall weeds are often found along walls, fences and hedges. Shaded areas under large trees will have sparser growth. Low-growing shrubs, like heather, tend to spread and tangle together in the wild with bare ground under them.

The Woodland Scenics items I used can be found in a good model railway shop; there are other makers too. The Silflor is harder to find, but again there are other makers. I've included in the 'Reference' chapter a good mail-order stockist that has a wide selection of makes.

Building a townscape base from a kit

Now let's look at a street scene kit from Verlinden, with my thanks to Historex Agents for providing it. Here we have a cobbled road corner with a badly damaged building. Although intended for the 1942 to 1945 period because it includes the steel packing tube for a 75mm German anti-tank gun shell, it can easily be adapted for an earlier setting by covering or disguising that part.

The building is in three sections with a separate low set of steps up to its entrance. It is made in resin but you need no special tools to work with this set, only a different glue. There is some 'flash' – a thin

The parts of the Verlinden resin base.

The resin has made a ridge around the bottom of the base. Instead of trying to cut or file it off, use felt pads to raise it and protect the furniture.

skin of resin – in the door and window openings but you only need your knife blade to remove this. The base and parts have been cast in one-piece moulds so have smooth, undetailed backs and the only problem is that the base's resin has shrunk so that its bottom is thinner than its edges, which make a ridge around it. See chapter 6 for the precautions needed when working with resin. Clear away any shavings, dust or little bits of resin and wash your hands when you finish working on the model in the same way that you tidy up and wash when working with plastic. Sanding a base this size to an even level is anyway rather hard to do – most people end up with a surface that is either domed in the middle or thinner at some edges than others, so it wobbles or has a slant

The building may not have a level bottom when built if you concentrate on lining up its brickwork correctly, so use Milliput to level its foundation.

instead of sitting flat and level. Instead, go to a furnishing or craft shop and buy some of the thick self-adhesive pads made to stick under ornaments so they don't scratch polished wooden surfaces. Stick one under each corner of the

base, then stick more on top of each one until it sits flat.

BUILDING THE BUILDING

Next, stick the building sections together. Use a two-part adhesive like Araldite for this as it has the strength you need for such large parts and dries slowly enough to let you adjust them so the lines of bricks meet at the same level around their corners. It also helps to fill any gaps! Squeeze equal amounts from the two tubes it comes in onto a piece of kitchen foil and mix them thoroughly. Then put the adhesive onto one joining

TOP RIGHT Don't forget to paint the bricks of the building's foundations!

BOTTOM RIGHT Here all the building's bricks have been picked out. There's no need to try and indicate the mortar between them yet.

surface and press the parts together. They will usually need five minutes for it to set. Test the sections against their locations on the base to make sure they are at the correct angle. Then mix more adhesive and attach the third section. Use your knife to pare off any adhesive that has squeezed out of the joints, after they are solid but before the glue has hardened completely.

The building edges may not meet evenly and the assembled building may not sit evenly on its location on the base. This is due to resin shrinkage, which can happen with large parts if they are cast in open-topped moulds. No problem, all you need to do is use two-part epoxy putty to fill any gaps. Take small pieces of each 'part' and roll them between your fingers into equal balls – it is important that both 'parts' are the same quantity when you mix them, so add a bit to the smaller ball if necessary. When your amounts are as near to equal as you can make them, roll the balls together into a long sausage. Double it over and repeat as many times as needed until the two colours have blended completely. Now it's ready to use.

Use your knife to press some into the gaps, making sure you

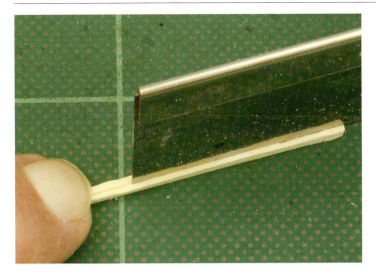

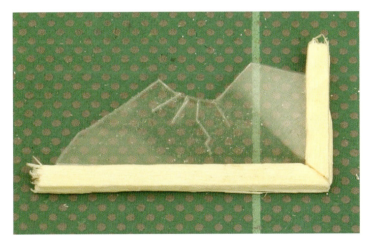

TOP LEFT The window frame pieces need a shallow slit sawn along them to represent the glazing groove.

BOTTOM LEFT The frame sections need mitred joints at their corners, and broken glass made by cutting clear plastic or acetate sheet.

keep the angled edge between the sections angled rather than flattened. It doesn't matter if there's more than you need in any place: you can cut off the surplus with your knife while it dries, which takes quite a long time. Remember to clean your knife when you finish, so the putty doesn't dry on it. When the building is rigid you can check how it sits on the base. If it isn't a good fit to the wall foundations just mix some more epoxy putty and make three sausages to run along the outer edges of the foundations. Press the building down onto them so it sits level, letting the putty squeeze out, and then do the same for the inner edges of the foundations. Cut away the excess putty level with the edges of the bricks. Now you have a good, solid building that sits properly on its foundations. You can still lift it off, which makes it much easier to do the painting, and you can decide whether to fix it permanently or leave it detachable so that storage is easier.

It's much easier to fix the steps when the building is complete and level on its foundations. You can attach them to the base or to the building and fill any gaps with epoxy putty. And while you have the putty by you, squeeze a bit as flat as you can and put it over that packing tube I mentioned earlier, on the left side of the roadway near the edge, to look like a bit of discarded blanket or a curtain blown out of a window.

Painting

Begin with white on the inside of the building, including the openings for the windows and door – I used Citadel's Skull White spray can. Next are base coats of any brick red you like on all the brickwork, including the foundations and fallen bricks on the base, and medium grey on the roadway and pavement areas. These are not just undercoats, you'll leave a lot of them showing, so make them cover properly.

ABOVE The window and doorframes are secured with carpenter's wood glue, like the floor pieces.

RIGHT Now you can paint the 'stone' parts of the building a pale grey, exposed mortar buff and the window and doorframes blue. Take the glass out of the frames first; you don't want paint on it because that would be out of scale.

Now pick out various bricks with different 'brick red' colours. Those can range from a dark red-brown to a quite orange shade, as many colours as you like, the important thing being to make sure that only a few bricks ever get the same colour next to each other. Cobblestones also come in a wide variety of colours, but you'll be putting a wash over them later so you can choose between picking them out in various shades of grey or simply dry-brushing their tops in a lighter grey.

Now you need to colour the stonework around the windows and door and the decorative line of stone around the building. I used a pale buff, common as the colour of stone for this kind of work, but you can opt for grey or even for white if you want to show it as painted. If you do decide to have it white you will need to pick out the damaged areas as the buff or grey of unpainted stone. Don't forget to paint the steps as well. Next is the darker buff of mortar, visible on the broken ends and top of the walls, with some brick red showing too. Use all these colours on the fallen brickwork too. Fallen bricks usually have some mortar left at an end or the top or bottom – you can vary how you show this, but most should have the buff colour on at least one surface. The buff of mortar dust should also go on the base itself where its texture shows as rough and dusty.

Creating a damaged interior

The inside of the building needs attention as well. A grand piano has fallen into the basement, but there are no floors for it to fall through so you will have to make your own 'broken floors'. Go to a craft shop, or any shop with a children's craft area, and look for the packs of wood aimed at youngsters. You should find both 'matchsticks' and 'lollipop sticks' and they are all you need. If a good hobby shop is nearer you can look there for packs of assorted balsa wood. Either way what you want are bits of wood that you can use for floorboards, the joists that they rest on, and window and doorframes. You will also need carpenter's white glue.

Start with the joists. Work out where the floors should be in your building and stick together bundles of 'matchsticks' to make the thicker timbers of the joists (if you're using balsa wood you want lengths about 10mm square). They won't be intact in a wrecked building, so line some of the joist sections that you make up on the insides of the walls with gaps between them and have others butted together to make longer 'remnants' — you'll cover the joints later so they won't show. Don't forget to have some running across the building as well as along its walls. Now come the floorboards, made with the 'lollipop sticks'. Use your saw to cut some at an angle to fit against the walls, and then break off the other ends — you want a broken appearance, not a saw-cut end. Glue them onto the joists with some next to each other and the rest as single remaining boards, making sure you cover any joints where your pieces of joist meet. Use masking tape to give a straight line between the joist sections and paint the exposed brickwork where the broken parts have fallen away, using several colours like the outside bricks. Paint some thin buff lines of mortar between the individual bricks too. A thin wash of a darkish brown on the tops and bottoms of the floorboards will bring out the grain of the wood to make them look better, but their broken ends must stay unpainted. The joists can either be given the same wash or, like mine, painted — if there was

Add a dusty wash to the whole base, the building and all the debris that's lying around.

no ceiling the exposed beams and joists were often painted either brown or black.

Final touches

One thing always seen in real life, but not included in most kits, is the framing in window and door openings. This is the surviving end of a building that has been on the fringe of an explosion, so it is obvious from the rest of the damage to it that a lot of this framing would have gone too. Adding some broken bits is quite straightforward. Take some 'matchsticks' and carefully saw along the tops of them to make the groove where the glass used to be, then snap them into pieces and glue them at random into the window openings. The bits of doorframe are 'matchsticks' without this groove. To make it look even more realistic, find some clear plastic – save the flat bits of bubble packs for this kind of thing – cut it into jagged shapes, and then glue them into the grooves. Finally, paint the frames in whatever colour you fancy.

Now you need to paint that piano and the other assorted bits

Use the dusty wash inside the building too, after painting the floor parts to look like well-used wood.

of debris on the base. Choose whatever colours you like for things like the 'old blanket' we've added, the oil drum, the oilcan and the bottles, but remember that most pianos were either gloss black or highly polished bare wood. The accordion in front of the door could be almost any gloss colour.

There's a rifle among the bits and pieces, and several empty shell cases, so paint them too. The last job is to add a dusty wash over the whole base and the building. Make a large batch, adding buff and grey paint to your thinner – the result of bombing or shellfire was plenty of mortar dust, so you need to aim for a dusty grey-buff shade. You can vary the wash while you apply it by adding more buff or grey.

Last, paint the edges of the base. Black is the usual choice, but you can have any colour you like. With that done you can add the building, put a tank on the base, and admire your work!

Working with etched metal

Some modellers avoid etched-metal sets because they have heard that this material can be difficult to handle. No, it isn't! I've already shown you the most basic type in the first Tiger built for this book, the items that are sometimes included in kits. Now it's time to look at the aftermarket sets that can add an incredible amount of extra detail to your models.

There are many aftermarket etched-metal manufacturers: Aber, Eduard, Part, Lion Roar and Voyager to name just a few. Some include resin parts or turned aluminium gun barrels, but I've already shown you how to deal with turned metal barrels and resin comes in the next chapter.

All of them can be shaped and assembled in the same way. But you do not have to use everything in a set. Sometimes parts that are really round are given as flat etched metal and it's better to use the round plastic part. Others may just be too fiddly or small to fold into shape until you are happy with simpler and larger etched parts.

Good sets are etched on both sides to provide bending lines. Older ones may not be, so you have to work out where to make some bends. Just scribe your own bending line – a small job that makes it much easier to bend the part.

Here I'm building the AFV Club M3A3 Stuart in Free French

A typical Eduard etched-metal set, this one for the Dragon SdKfz 251.

The contents of a typical Eduard etched-metal set – instructions, frets and a very neat colour-printed instrument dial sheet to go with the instrument panel provided.

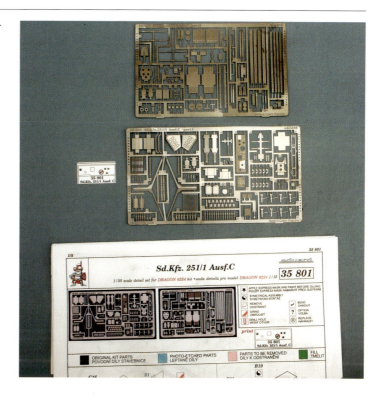

Eduard's set of masks for the Academy Achilles includes ones cut from masking film and also an etched-metal mask. I peeled back one of the 'film' masks so you can see that this type actually gives two options – use the block with the star removed to paint a white star, or paint a white patch and put the star on it before painting the model in its camouflage colour. The 'film' type can be used several times if you're careful in removing them.

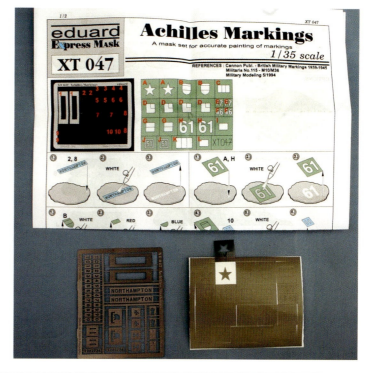

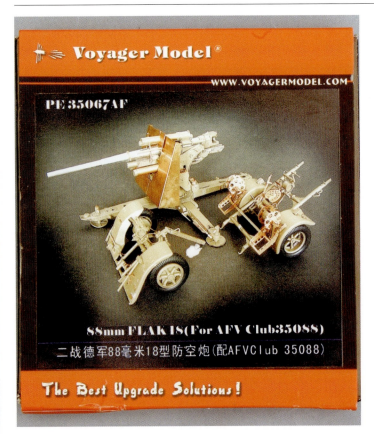

Voyager makes a number of good etched sets.

markings, so before I get into the 'working with etched metal' section I'll show you the extra work I did. This particular tank was photographed in Summer 1944 in a clean condition, as if prepared for a parade in liberated Paris, so I have left it unweathered. The amount of weathering you apply to any model is entirely up to you, and many modellers like a clean appearance and don't weather their models at all. There's nothing wrong with that: your model is your model so no one should tell you how much it should be weathered.

TOOLS FOR WORKING WITH ETCHED PARTS

You will already have most of the basic tools – knife, file and steel ruler. You'll also need small smooth-jawed pliers to hold small parts while you clean them up. Some jobs are made much easier with special tools and others are very difficult without them so let's look at those.

A bending tool is very useful – you can make all the bends without one, but using it makes it much easier to handle multiple bends. There are several makes, and they work by using a hand screw to clamp a shaped head onto a flat base with the etched fret between them. You position the head on each bending line and simply slip a blade under the metal to bend it up. All these tools come with a straight edge to let you make long bends and 'fingers' to slip inside box shapes so you can do their sides, and are very easy to use. Whichever make you choose buy the medium size, because the short ones cannot help you with long bends and the very long ones aren't needed for tank models. Many of these tools come with a long steel blade, like a ruler with one edge bevelled, to make the bends themselves. If yours doesn't you can slip the tip of your knife along under the edge of the metal to raise it slightly and then use your steel ruler to do the actual bending. It's important to bend the whole length of metal at the same time so you don't end up with some areas bent more than others.

For 'tube' shapes you'll find another choice of tools. The Small Shop EU has a Brass-Assist rolling set, a selection of metal rollers with a machined metal base to fit them. The part is placed in a groove on the base and the roller pressed down onto it to begin the U-shape, then to complete a tube you slip the roller inside the tube and roll it on the padded back of

TRACK PROBLEMS AND HOW TO DEAL WITH THEM

The tracks provided are the flexible type, which can be painted in exactly the same way as the multi-part tracks we've looked at before. Some manufacturers give them in a plastic that can be glued with ordinary plastic cement, but others still give tracks in a plastic that cannot be cemented successfully. For these you use the locating pins and holes at each end of a track run. Test the fit of the tracks before you fix them together, because sometimes they are too long or too short. If they are too long you can shorten them a bit by cutting off a link at one or both ends – there are normally at least two rows of pins and holes to let you do this. If they are too short, or only just long enough, they may strain your model's suspension so that wheels start to pop off. There are two solutions to this. One is to superglue the tracks to the wheels, leaving a gap between their ends either under overhanging trackguards or on a base with plenty of 'mud' or 'grass' to hide it.

The other solution is to buy aftermarket tracks. Some resin ones need superglue to hold them together, while others will snap together. There are metal tracks with holes into which you push wire 'track pins' just like full-size tracks, and there are plastic and metal tracks that come with a former for assembly. Sometimes they have several parts for each link (even some kits have these) but all you need is to be sparing with the cement so you don't stick them all solid before you can put them round the wheels. The white-metal tracks with a former are quite easy to assemble. You simply put the links on the former and press down the jaws of each one around the cast-in 'pin' on the next link.

The individual link tracks do have advantages. American tanks had 'live' track, with a tendency to curl up because of the way it was made. This kept it from sagging between the return rollers. German,

Modelkasten makes tracks for a variety of tanks, often with extra parts, like this set for Tamiya's T-55, to modify the kit sprockets. Their 'workable' sets include separate track pins to join the links, as shown here, and all you do after fixing them is cut off the 'handle' of each pin. The result is a track that droops just like the real thing. They also make non-working tracks that are simply cemented together.

British and Soviet tanks had 'dead' tracks without this curl to keep them up, so sagged onto the roadwheels or between the return rollers. If you build a model German tank with flexible plastic track you will need to reproduce this sag by supergluing the tracks to the wheels. Another way is to drill holes through the hull from one side to the other and push stiff wire through them to hold the tracks down. This is not really successful and the wire can be much too noticeable, so it's best to either ignore the problem or try out some aftermarket tracks. Their disadvantage is price, as some can cost more than the kit you put them on – though the satisfaction of having tracks that look right makes up for that. This kit's tracks are the right length and need so sag, so no problems here!

Replacing solid headlamp lenses

This kit's headlamp lenses, like those in many kits, are moulded as solid green plastic with their rims around them, but simply painting the lenses silver will not look very convincing. The answer is to cut the locating lugs off their backs and, while they are still on their moulding sprue, make a hole though each one leaving just the rim to take an aftermarket reflective lens. This is easy. Cut off the locating tab on the back, and then use your knifepoint to mark the dead centre of each lens and twirl it there to make a little hole. The hole will keep your drill bit steady while you drill through the plastic – a 2.5mm bit will do for this kit and most others with standard US Army headlamps. Trim any remaining snags of plastic away from the insides of the rims and then cut them free from the sprue and cement them to the lamp bodies. After fixing the lamps to the tank and completing painting, but before weathering it, you can pop an aftermarket lens into each one. Here I used 2.5mm lenses with reflective backs from Resicast but there are other makes. Some have a self-adhesive backing but those without it only need a drop of white glue to hold them in place.

The headlamp lenses are moulded in solid green.

Each lens has a locating lug on the back. Cut it off.

Make a pilot hole in the centre by twisting the tip of your knife blade.

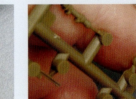

Open the hole out with a 2.5mm drill bit – you need that pilot hole to keep the centre of the bit in the centre of the lens.

ABOVE Here's the rim fitted to the lamp body.

RIGHT A real reflective lens looks much better than silver paint over the green plastic would ever do. Fix it in place after you've painted the model but before weathering it – headlamps get dirty just like the rest of a tank.

the base. Mission Models also has a rolling tool, the Multi Tool, in two sizes. Both combine several diameters and your cutting mat works well as their base for rolling.

I find both these tools very handy, and use both of them. One thing that you need to do for successful rolling is anneal the etched part first. This is simple: hold one end of it in your pliers and heat it till it glows, wait till you can turn it round without burning your fingers, and heat the other end. Let it cool naturally, don't put it in cold water or the softening will be reversed. Some modellers use a candle for the heating but these you must remember to blow them out after use and, if knocked, they can tip over and set light to things. I prefer to use a throwaway cigarette lighter, which goes out when you let go of it so is not a fire hazard.

The final useful addition to your toolbox is Mission Models' Micro Chisel, a steel shaft with a rubber sleeve for a good grip and a very sharp tip at its business end. The standard 2mm tip that comes with it is just what you need for removing small details to be replaced by etched parts.

METAL RODS AND WIRE

Several tools give ways of bending metal rods or wire to make grab handles or US-type tie-downs, so I'll look at another of those while we're talking about special tools. Mission Models' Grab Handler is designed to make grab handles but is also excellent for tie-downs. It is a pair of shaped jaws held together by a handscrew, and to use it you simply put wire between the jaws at the marker for the size you want,

A bending tool is much easier to use for parts that must have a bend. Here I'm using the 5.5in. Hold and Fold and preparing to bend the bolt strip for the air vent on the next model.

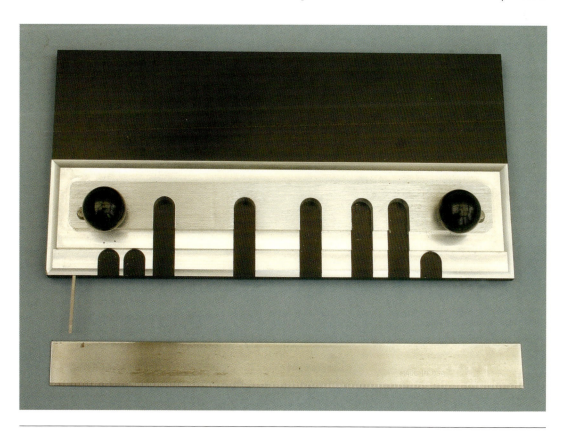

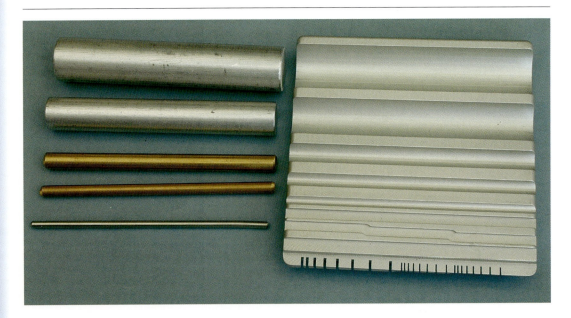

The Brass-Assist tool is very easy to use.

tighten the screw, and bend the wire's ends down. To cut the rod you'll need a small wire cutter, but if you intend to cut steel wire you must make certain that it has hardened jaws. Unhardened jaws can cope with copper or brass wire, but steel will spoil them. You can buy brass and steel wire in most good hobby shops in several diameters. Copper wire is much softer, so easier to shape as you want it. The best way to get copper wire is to buy short lengths of electric flex in different sizes and strip off their plastic insulation. Take a look at the end of the flex before you buy, the exposed copper wire inside may be a bundle of very fire wires or a single thicker one and you can choose flex with the wire thickness you want.

So, on with the model

With the basic building done you can add the etched set, and here I've used the one made by Eduard for the M3A3 kit. It gives a lot of extra details, but there are some etched parts in the kit itself and you can use these if you prefer. The 'spares' are handy for practising before you start on the ones you want to use.

The first step is to add the rear exhaust screen. Hold the etched fret down on your cutting mat with your fingers positioned so that you hold the fret flat and also hold down the part you're cutting from it. It's best to make this a habit even with fairly large parts like this one – the smaller the part the easier it is for it to spring away as you cut it free, and the further it is likely to bounce from wherever it lands. Now cut with your knife blade where the part is connected to the fret. Not right against the part, that often warps it, but leaving a small stub of the fret attached to it. Just cut down, don't try to cut along the stub because that's also a good way to warp the part. The metal is thin so your blade will cut through it.

Now hold the part with your pliers so that you can file gently along the stub until it has gone – not across it, as that is another way to warp it. You can straighten any accidental creases in the metal by squeezing them flat with your pliers. Now put it where it has to go and make sure you see which way round it fits. Many etched parts have right and wrong sides, so look to see where raised details on them go. Fixing a part needs superglue. The thin, runny type is

The Grab Handler clamps the wire between graduated jaws like this.

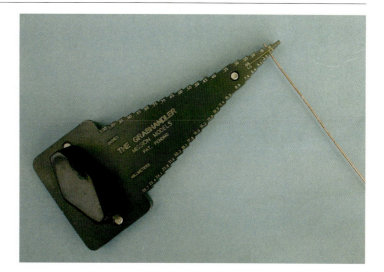

With the Brass-Assist select the slots for the size of handle and fit the wire into them. You have to use soft copper wire for this as brass rod is too stiff unless you anneal it very well first to soften it.

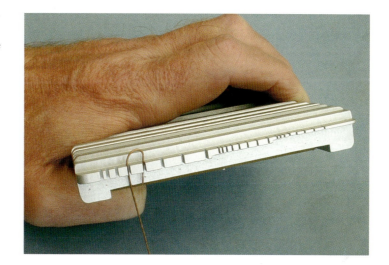

Here are the results from the Grab Handler on the left, already cut to length, and the Brass-Assist on the right not yet to cut.

good for parts like this screen; take a drop on the tip of a wooden toothpick or cocktail stick and dot it where the part will go – for longer parts such as this one you need to get it at least on each corner and in several places along each side. It stays good for several seconds but you do need to work quickly. Don't put it on the part unless there's no other way to apply it, you don't want to stick yourself or your modelling tools to the part! Make sure you have your debonder handy in case this does happen, or nail varnish remover which works nearly as well. Now gently put the part into place,

Hold the part with your pliers and file along it to remove the tiny stubs. Don't file across it or you'll bend the thin metal.

making sure it is aligned correctly and the right way round. Press it down. Done!

If you accidentally misalign it, or see that it has not attached properly, you can take it off. Slip your knife blade under an edge and lever gently, moving the blade along the joint. Then tweak off the superglue residue from both the plastic and the etched part, because many superglues do not stick to themselves very well and anyway the extra glue will stop the part from sitting flat on the plastic. Straighten it if necessary before refixing it.

Shaping parts

I often use my pliers to shape small parts, holding them at their etched bending lines and simply pressing the adjacent section up against the pliers. This is what I learnt to do long before bending tools were invented, but you'll find it better to use a tool. The principle is the same, clamping the part at its bending line and pressing the next bit up. All kinds of parts need this, with tool clamps a typical example. German clamps actually have a series of bends, so their ends meet, but some etched ones come as separate parts and can even open and close. Most non-German tanks had their tools held by straps that were secured to the tanks by 'tie-downs'. These are bigger versions of the eyes of hook-and-eye fastenings. Some sets give the straps with their tie-downs attached, so you just need to bend the strap up at each side of the tie-down, superglue it to the tank, put the tool in place and bend the

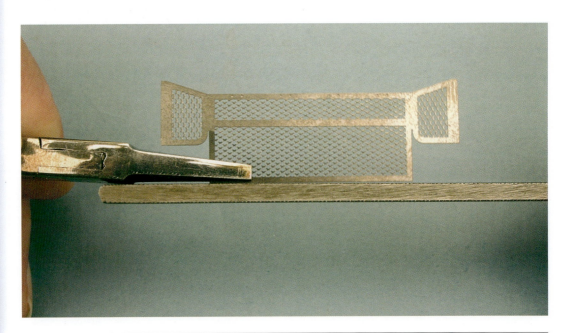

strap so that its end goes through its buckle. Other sets give you the tie-downs by themselves, so you can either leave them empty or make straps from thin paper to go through them. These have a double bend to make at each side. That's only a slight complication, once you are used to making single bends it's easy to make a second one in the other direction. Start at one end and make the first bend then turn the part round and make the second, move it along in your tool to make the third, and finally take it out and replace it at its very end to make the last one.

Headlamp guards, on the other hand, can be tricky because they have round tops. This is where a rolling tool is very useful. Anneal the metal and put it in the appropriate groove of the Brass-Assist, straight and centred on it, then press down with the roller to make the U-shape; check which groove to use by comparing them with the plastic guard from the kit. If you use a Multi Tool just put the centre of the guard on the appropriate section of the tool and press down each side. Whichever tool you use, you may find that the legs of the guard are no longer flat. Simply squeeze them flat with your pliers.

With parts like these you have a very small gluing surface, just the ends of the guard's legs. Thin superglue has nothing to hold onto, so the part can be knocked

STRETCHING SPRUE FOR RADIO AERIALS

You'll often hear of stretched sprue: it's an easy way of making a thin rod with a taper, which is just what most radio aerials are. Cut a length of the plastic sprue that you've removed all the parts from, at least 10cm or 4in. long so you don't risk burning your fingers. Hold it 5cm above a flame. If you are using a small candle hold it at both ends and pull gently and slowly when the centre starts sagging so it stretches in the middle. When you have a piece that's long enough and thin enough, take it away from the heat and let it cool while you blow out the candle. Then cut out the section you want. If you use a throwaway lighter you can only hold one end of the sprue. Just hold it at the same distance above the flame and wait for it to soften in the middle and bend down. Quickly drop the lighter, it will go out automatically, and pull both ends. You won't get such a long stretched section, but it will still be quite long enough for you to cut what you need from it.

off the model very easily. Use gel superglue instead. Put a drop on the bottom of each leg (this is an exception to putting it on the model) and set it in place. The superglue spreads a little way up each leg to hold it firmly, and looks like the weld used to attach the real guard to its tank.

Some etched sets include perforated outer jackets for machine guns. These are usually very thin, so you don't need to anneal them and can simply roll them to shape. The smallest diameter rod of the Multi Tool is ideal for this. Just place the part at the edge of your cutting mat, press the rod down hard and roll it from side to side on the part. It will slowly take up a curve, and if you keep on rolling it will curve right

round into a tube. Now cut off the plastic machine gun barrel and drill a hole into the body of the gun where it was to take a suitable piece of plastic rod to represent the barrel inside its new jacket. Glue the rod into place and cut it to length, 1 mm shorter than the original plastic barrel, then paint it black because you won't be able to reach it later. Now drill a hole into the muzzle of the original barrel, cut off the 1mm tip, and superglue it to the tip of the jacket. Done!

All these jobs can be done without the special tools, as many modellers did long before the tools were invented. Your pliers and steel ruler can bend almost any part to shape, and you can use your stirring rod or the handles of various-sized paintbrushes to form

U-shapes and tubes. The special tools make it a whole lot easier, but if cash is short don't feel that you can't handle etched parts without buying them.

More about the model

Unfortunately the etched grouser racks that go on the sides of the turret are the wrong size – don't try to use them because the grousers don't fit them. Use the plastic parts instead, and attach the grousers by working from one end of the rack to the other because they can't fit otherwise. The spare track racks on the back of the hull are also not quite right. You will need to lengthen them a bit and add a bottom piece as shown in my photographs. The turret shouldn't have a round hole in its top; this was a hatch for signal flags to be waved through, and should be filled because it was rarely opened.

TOP Form curves around a suitable rod – this is a Tamiya paint stirrer. Special tools make this kind of job much easier but this is how we used to do it before the tools were invented.

BOTTOM Sharp bends are made along the etched bending lines using pliers and a flat surface like your steel ruler or a knife blade.

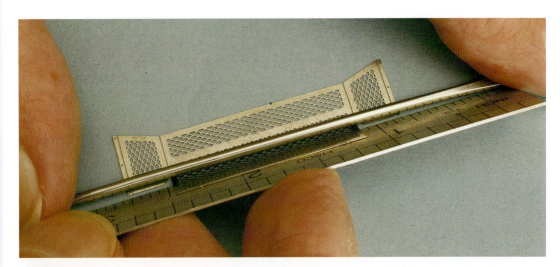

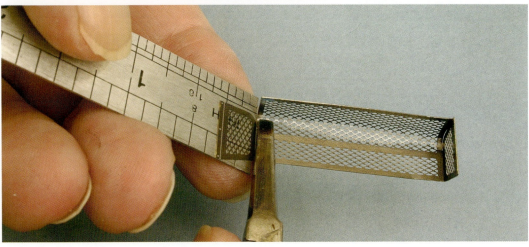

Use a roller larger than the finished size you want to begin the shaping.

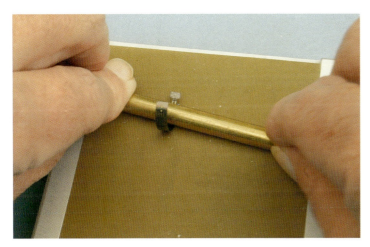

And a smaller one to roll the part to its final shape on the soft back of the tool.

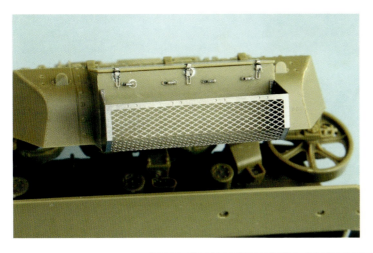

This is the rear stowage basket and its etched tie-downs.

The completed turret interior. The ammunition belt is fiddly to fit because you have to curve it sideways but this is how the real one fitted.

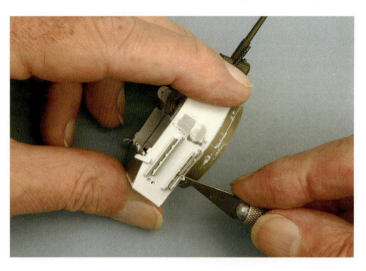

If you need to remove unwanted plastic parts cut away a bit at a time; cutting too deeply risks disaster. Here I'm getting ready to fit the Eduard grouser racks that turned out to be too short to hold the grousers.

Final touches

I used Tamiya's spraycan TS-28, Olive Drab 2, for this model, masking and painting the parts and applying the decals just as before. However, the large French division signs for the sides are a bit too large so you need to cut them at top and bottom to match the size of the hull where they fit. Measure the correct size with your steel ruler and make sure you trim the same amounts at top and bottom so the diamond interior stays centred. Then, after applying the decals, use your 000 brush to paint a thin white line at top and bottom.

The etched spare track mounts are very nice, but as you can see the U-shaped one is not wide enough to let the track pin fit inside it.

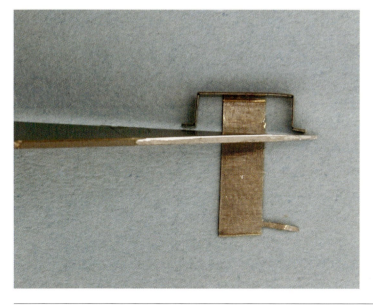

The new mount also needs a bottom; here I'm checking its size against the Eduard etched mount.

KITS WITH RESIN AND WHITE-METAL PARTS

Resin cuts in just the same way as polystyrene and can be sawed, filed, drilled and filled with exactly the same techniques that you are already using. Resin can't be glued with plastic cements, but superglues and two-part epoxy glues are ideal for it.

FIRST, LET'S LOOK AT RESIN

You may have heard stories about how difficult it is to work with resin and how dangerous this medium can be. Well, they're rubbish! Modern resin conversions, update sets and kits are no more difficult to build than their polystyrene cousins, and not hazardous unless you are one of the few who is particularly sensitive to their dust.

Nevertheless a wise precaution is to make a habit of wearing a high-quality dust mask if you are going to file, saw or sandpaper resin. Breathing too much dust of any kind is bad for you, so minimize your chances of breathing it.

But I must say that I have been working with resin kits since they first appeared and have never had any problems because I don't inhale the dust. In fact I avoid sanding it as much as possible and so should you.

Because it is mixed from two constituents that generate heat

while they set it does sometimes have bubbles in it – usually called 'air bubbles', though they're not what you get by stirring air into a mixture. Sometimes they break the surface and need to be filled, and sometimes they're hidden inside a part so only need to be dealt with if you cut down to them while trimming it.

Kit and accessory manufacturers cast resin in several ways. The oldest, rare nowadays unless you cast your own parts, is an open-topped mould with the resin simply poured into it and left to set. Another is the 'squash mould', where two open-topped moulds are filled and then squashed together before the resin sets. Both of these leave a good amount of cleaning up to do, either a surplus where the mould was filled or flash around the joint of the squash mould. Good resin kits are made with more advanced techniques that produce parts on casting plugs that you simply cut them from just like plastic parts on their sprue.

CUTTING THE PARTS FROM THEIR CASTING BLOCKS

Large parts often come with a large casting plug, needed to make sure that enough resin is flowed into the part. You will often need to saw these away, wearing your mask, but there won't be many like this in any particular kit. Inspect the part first and make sure that you know where it ends and the casting block begins – first appearances can be deceptive so double-check; then saw as close as you can to the part, but not right against it. When the part is free from its block you can trim off the remaining resin with a sharp knife blade. Gentle filing will deal with what's left, but next you must sweep up and dispose of all the dust and bits before they fly all over the place – as I wrote above, they will cling to the model. I usually start a resin model by doing this job for all the large parts over newspaper, which I then fold over the dust and throw away.

The large parts are easy to identify, but smaller ones can be

Use the part's overhang of the block as a saw guide. Cut between parts on a single block to make access easier.

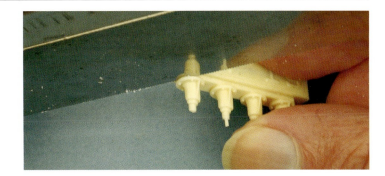

Sometimes a casting block partly encloses the part. Saw it away in sections.

Some casting blocks can be removed safely by scoring the parting line and snapping them away from the part.

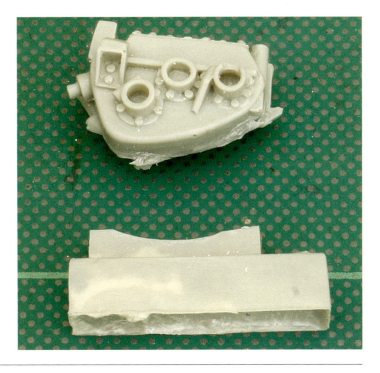

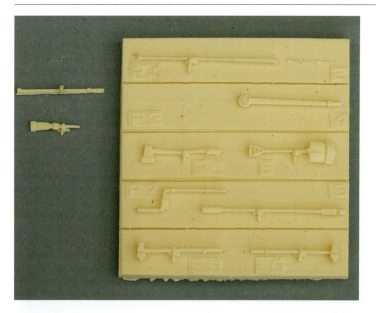

TOP Formations' resin tool set is a good example of parts cast onto a single block as well as being a good set of US-type tools. Simply slice under each one and clean up its bottom, sawing the block apart as necessary to reach each tool.

BOTTOM The Eduard etched part for the side panel does not have bend lines at the bottom so won't bend cleanly. To avoid this appearance, scribe your own bending line on its back.

replacements if parts are broken, missing, or defective because the resin had not quite set before the kit was packed, or a bubble was invisible inside the casting block but emerges to spoil the part when you cut it free.

Small parts are usually attached in groups to long blocks. Many can simply be scored at their attachment points with the tip of your knife blade until they come free, but take care to score on both sides so the part isn't damaged by leaving a bit of itself behind. Watch also for multiple attachment points – free the part at its smallest or weakest attachment first and work up to the most solid: that way you won't find that the first point to come loose snaps the whole part away with damage elsewhere.

Some makers put the parts on small casting blocks on top of the main ones instead of providing a 'stem' that you can score or cut through. I find it best to saw through the main block between each part and then to saw gently under the small block, finishing off

awkward to tell apart. Some manufacturers provide part numbers on the casting blocks, keyed to the instructions, and others give you an illustrated parts list with the numbers so you have to sort out which is which and pencil its number onto it. Good manufacturers take great care in their packing and provide

by cutting around the part to remove most of its block and then simply using my knife to trim away any remaining excess resin. This reduces the amount of dust from sawing as well as the risk of damaging the parts.

You can also find parts attached to the tops of large oblong blocks. Cut them between the parts and either continue as I've just described or score under the parts to remove them.

The most awkward casting blocks are those attached to the bottoms of large parts like hull bottoms. Depending on the thickness of these blocks there are several ways to remove them. The oldest is to use wet-and-dry sandpaper taped to a flat surface and move the part against the paper with water under it to keep the dust down. Use a figure-of-eight motion and reverse the direction frequently, as well as changing which way round you hold the part. The drawback to this is that it is very hard to keep your sanded surface flat and level, but very easy indeed to take more off the edges than the middle (so you end up with a dome instead of a flat bottom) or more off one side or end than the others (so the bottom is sloped). Some modellers use a motorized flatbed sander instead, but this produces a lot of dust and can still have the same results.

I prefer other methods. The best is to use your modelling saw blade, or an ordinary fretsaw if the block is large, to saw all round along the part where it overhangs the block (which it usually does). If you saw the four sides first and then the corners, taking care to keep the saw level with the block, these saw cuts will guide the blade while you continue towards its centre. You can then file away any remaining unevenness. If the block is wider than the part you can do the same

Air bubbles

Bubbles often show just a surface translucency to reveal that there's one inside the resin. There's no need to do anything about those. But some do break the surface, or are exposed while you remove the casting block, and need to be filled. Use the tip of your knife to press filler into small to medium-sized bubbles. It can be easier to fill very small bubbles if you deliberately make them bigger with your drill, and it's definitely easier to fill a bubble that only just breaks the surface if you open its top up so you can pack filler into the whole bubble. Some modellers use the kind of liquid filler sold by Gunze Sangyo as 'Mr Filler' for these tiny bubbles. You just brush it over them so it can sink into the holes, and file it to restore the surface afterwards. Larger bubbles need a different treatment. Use two-part epoxy filler, such as Milliput, which will adhere to the resin surface. After it has set you can cut and file it to shape, which makes it very handy for bubbles in

such places as the corners of trackguards. An alternative that I often use is to put superglue into the bubble and then dip the part into a pile of ordinary talcum powder. The powder will act as a filler for the superglue and bulk it out, and you can repeat the process as needed until the bubble is completely filled and then file or carve the excess away. Even major bubbles can be dealt with by these methods, so if you find one of the rare large bubbles that have escaped quality control you can usually fix it. Break the surface on the inside of the part, where it won't be seen after assembly, but keep the outside intact. Use superglue and talc to stabilize the outside surface so that it doesn't flex when you prod it but keeps its proper shape. Now you can either continue with superglue and talc or use epoxy filler to restore the part's thickness. If this seems too tricky just ask the manufacturer for a replacement.

BROKEN PARTS

Parts can break, just like those in polystyrene kits, but it's simple to repair them. If one is broken when you take it out of the box check carefully among all the little bits and find the missing piece (if it isn't there at all but was lost before packing, contact the manufacturer for a replacement part). Hold it in place against the part to test how to press it into place. Now apply a little thin superglue – capillary action will suck it into the crack. Once it has set you can clean up the surface with a file. The same method will repair cracked parts that haven't actually split in two: just put a drop of superglue on the crack while you hold it firmly together.

but will need first to cut away the overhang so you can see where the block ends and the part begins. The last alternative is to use a motor tool such as the ones made by Dremel, with a grinding head instead of a drill bit, and grind away the block. This works well but also produces a lot of dust.

DEALING WITH PROBLEMS

You will sometimes find resin parts that have warps, damage or air bubbles that escaped the eyes of quality control, and sometimes parts get damaged in the post or warped by warmth in storage at a shop or at home. So let's look at how to deal with these problems.

First, warps. Resin is affected by heat, especially under pressure from other parts in the box. Check inside the box when you get it for parts that are pressing against each other, and for any that have been tightly wrapped as protection. Re-

arrange the contents to eliminate pressure and undo any tight wrappings! If you do find that parts have warped a little the problem is easy to correct. Fill a suitable dish with hot – not boiling – water, deep enough to cover the part. Then put the part in and wait a little while. Use your tweezers instead of your fingers to take the part out, as the water should still be hot. Test by pressing against the warp: if the resin has been warmed enough you

will be able to reshape the part and get rid of the warp. If it resists reshaping, put it into a fresh lot of hot water and let it sit a bit longer until you can 'unwarp' it. Flat parts can be pressed against a flat surface to reshape them, and you can tape them firmly against something like a piece of glass and heat them with a hairdryer instead of hot water.

Unfortunately some warps will never respond to this treatment, because the resin set warped instead of flat. Heat will straighten this kind of warp for a while but it will always come back. The only thing you can do with this fault is to contact the manufacturer and ask for a replacement – good firms will always provide one, though they may ask you to send the faulty part back first.

A MODEL USING RESIN PARTS

For this model I turned the Academy M3A1 kit, which has a

SHAPING RESIN TRACKS WITH HEAT

You can also use heat to shape parts as you want them, particularly resin tracks that come in lengths to be bent around a model's wheels. Never try to bend cold track, as it will break! Place it on the sprocket or idler and use a hairdryer to warm it until it starts to bend, then gently persuade it to meet the roadwheels. Only use as much heat as is needed to get it to bend, not a full-scale blast on the hottest setting or you may find other parts warp from the heat, or even get blown loose to fly across the room!

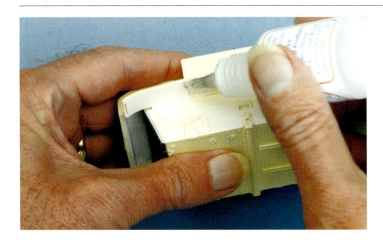

To fix large parts like these you can apply thin superglue straight from the tube. It will run along the joint and fix them together if you apply a bit at intervals along the parts. Wipe off any surplus with a tissue before it dries.

riveted hull, into the more common welded hull type using the very nice resin upper and lower hull sets from Formations Models and the Eduard etched-metal set. This let me use the kit's decals for one of the US Marine Corps tanks on Bougainville, which had welded hulls. Apart from the absence of rivets their important difference from the riveted hulls is the rounded end to their engine decks. Formations' sets provide complete new upper and lower hulls with much better details than Academy's, the upper one sized to fit the Academy lower hull for simplicity if you don't want to buy both sets and the lower hull with extra details inside and outside. I also added an aftermarket gun barrel to show you how to adapt the kit to take it. My special thanks go to Formations Models for providing the resin sets I used for this model.

The Academy kit comes with interior parts which I improved with Eduard's interior set. These particular US Marine tanks carried the fuel drop tanks provided by Academy, so I corrected those and added their missing fuel pipes and release cables. This isn't really difficult, see my photos.

Once the resin lower hull is cleaned up you can simply follow the set's instructions to fit out its interior. Many etched sets that include interior parts give an

Cut the case deflector parts off the gun breech and glue them together to help you gauge its width and make the metal one match it. Its ends are not opposite each other; one side is longer than the other.

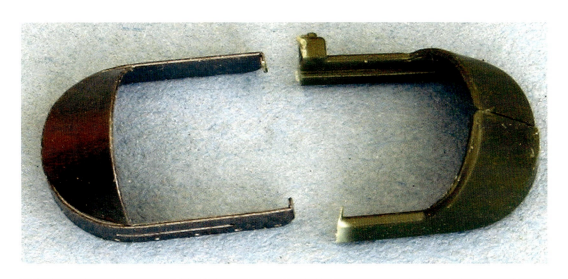

Make strips of track like this by adding one block and connector at a time and securing them with a touch of cement, then turning the strip round and adding the connectors for the other side. Make short strips, press them on a flat surface so they're flat and straight, and join them together when they're nearly dry to complete a top or bottom run.

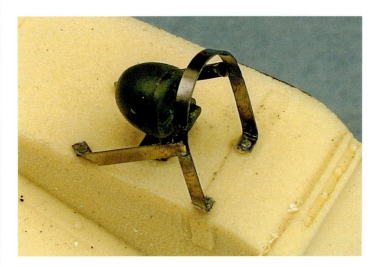

Attach the headlamp guard on the strip in front of the lamp, right against the inner edge of the trackguard. Its supports fit like this into the recesses on the guard.

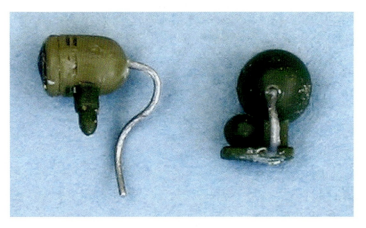

Cables go into the backs of the siren and each lamp like this. The best source of thin wire is inside an electric flex.

Roll copper wire under your ruler to straighten it.

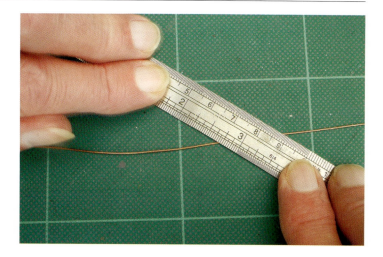

The port lamp cable runs like this.

And this is how the starboard lamp and siren cables run.

To fit an etched screen you need to drill into the old one so you can cut it away, then smooth the edges.

This is the completed assembly showing how it needs to be notched to fit the turret ring.

Pare away the straps and mounts of the fuel drums a little bit at a time, then finish with a file.

Here are the air filters in place. Note the shape and position of the fuel drum mounts.

Academy's tanks are the right size and nearly the right shape but lack their filler caps and have no fuel pipes. Assemble them as usual, then file off the bands round them and round off the corners of their ends – not to domes, leave their centres flat. Next, make two cuts, 4mm apart and 4mm long, in the middle of their tops. Slice between these to get a flat surface and cut a section from the sprue to make the filler cap that goes in its centre.

Now you need to add their canvas carrying handles with narrow strips of paper 25mm long – they don't have to be flat, photographs show them flopping around. On the bottom of each tank drill a 1.5mm hole opposite the filler cap and use your knife to make a trench leading from it to one side for the fuel pipe.

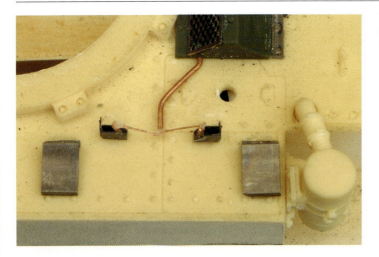

This is how the cable releases for the drums fit. Just drill into the side of the engine grille and add the wires.

Now you add the correct filler cap arrangement to the tank's engine deck. Use Academy parts E14 and E23 with the peg cut off and reattached at the top. The armoured caps will be open for the droptank pipes to reach the fuel tanks, of course. To make those pipes you need a 25mm length of rubber tube (I bought mine from Accurate Armour) with one end superglued into the hole under the droptank.

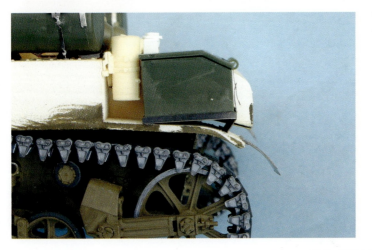

This is how the box and its etched support fits on the trackguard.

The completed model Stuart.

instrument panel. You need to pare or file away the detail on the plastic panel and fix the etched one over it, but the advantage is that you get instrument dials as part of the etched set. This saves you from painting the dials! They come either as photo transparencies, whose backs you paint white, or as printed dials on paper that will need a drop of gloss varnish on each dial to provide its 'glazed' appearance. The only disadvantage of etched instrument panels is that the 'knobs' on them are always flat. Cut the knobs from the plastic panel and superglue them to the etched one. You need to paint the etched panel before putting the dials behind it but it's worth the effort for the realistic appearance.

Etched screens always look much better than moulded ones, but to fit them you have to remove the moulded one first. This is easy. Drill holes around the area to be removed, just inside its edge and as close together as you can, and cut between the holes so you can pop out the piece. Then tidy up the edges with your knife while checking for the etched screen to fit, and fix it in place. You can make holes in anything with this technique, whether to replace a moulded screen with etch or just to open a hatch that's moulded solid.

WEATHERING WITH PASTEL PIGMENTS

This tank had a white interior with black leather upholstery for its seats, black rubber grips on the controls, and olive drab ammunition boxes and main gun. Being white it will look very garish and unrealistic if you don't weather it – tank crews don't wipe their boots before climbing in! My subject was photographed on Bougainville, a Pacific island with a reddish soil, so I used MIG Productions P031 Vietnam Earth pigment, a reddish brown that's good for this type of soil. Dip an old brush into it and brush it in all the places where dirt would collect (not forgetting the seats) and heavily for the places where dirty boots would deposit it and in all the corners. If you do this over a clean sheet of paper you can turn the tank over and tap its bottom to drop any surplus onto it, then tip it from the paper back into the pot to avoid wasting any! Add a few metallic scuffmarks with steel-grey paint for areas of heavy wear. You can use the same method to weather the outside when the model is finished. Several other pigment ranges are available.

I added an Eduard turned metal gun barrel to this model so I could show you how to fit one when the kit is not engineered to take it. The first step is to remove the plastic barrel, which in this case has a recuperator cylinder under it that you needed to keep. Slice between the barrel and the cylinder with a sharp knife until they are completely separate, and then saw through where the barrel joins its breech (in this kit the barrel ends inside the turret, but for many models you will only have to

MAKING NEW GEAR LEVERS

It's easy to break delicate parts like gear levers while you clean them up whether they are resin, white metal or plastic. Put the parts together and measure their length, then cut a piece of brass rod to match and bend it to the same shape. There are several ways to make the knob on the end of a gear lever: you can dip the end into epoxy glue or thick superglue several times and let it build up into a knob of the right size, but my favourite method is

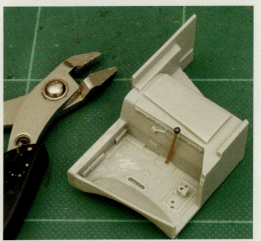

Gear levers can break, but you can make one with brass rod filed to fit the slit of an anglers' split shot.

much simpler. Use fishermen's split shot weights, available from any anglers' shop. I have a pack of assorted sizes, made from imitation lead so not toxic. Slip your knife into the split to open it out, pop it onto the end of the rod, press it shut and secure it with superglue (which also fills the split). This is often easier than cleaning up the kit part! If your original lever has a 'boot' at its bottom end just drill into that and fix the replacement into it, then add the boot to the cab floor.

The painted cab interior parts.

remove the part outside the gun mantlet). Clean up the exposed end, then drill into it to accept the locating peg on the metal barrel. Finally, put a little thin superglue on the peg and push it into the hole, making sure the barrel is straight.

Now for a model with white-metal parts

This model is Accurate Armour's Deacon, a British self-propelled 6-pdr anti-tank gun mounted on the chassis of a Matador truck and given armour. It is what modellers call a 'multimedia' kit, because it includes several different materials – in this case resin, etched brass and white metal.

White metal should not be confused with any lead alloy. It is a special blend with no toxic ingredients, so you don't need to worry about lead poisoning. However, as with resin or plastic dust you don't want it all over the place or on your model so clean up after any filing or sawing. It will saw and file easily, and you can scrape or pare it with a knife. Superglue will stick white metal, but two-part epoxy glue or soldering are essential for large, heavy parts.

You may sometimes find that parts are not completely cast, or misshaped because their mould was deformed, but they don't warp because white metal is relatively insensitive to heat. Makers will provide replacements just as with resin parts. Beware, however, of 'white-metal' kits that contain suspiciously soft parts – they may be cast from solder, which will melt if you try to solder them together! No good manufacturer nowadays uses this shortcut, but some older kits that you may still find did use solder for small, delicate castings.

Most of this kit is resin, which I need not discuss again. Like most 'truck' kits it is built on a chassis. This one is a single piece, but sometimes they're built up from separate sides with cross-pieces to connect them. Either way it is essential that the chassis is level, so check for any warps and correct

Two-part epoxy glues are best for parts that take any weight or strain.

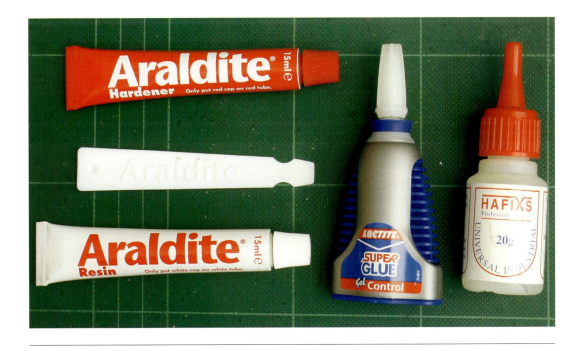

RIGHT Put same-sized blobs of each epoxy on a bit of kitchen foil and mix them. I shaped a piece of sprue as a mixer and application tool.

BELOW The chassis bottom with the front springs, axle and drive shaft in place.

BOTTOM Here's the completed chassis. The fuel tank has to be mounted low down, not right on the chassis side.

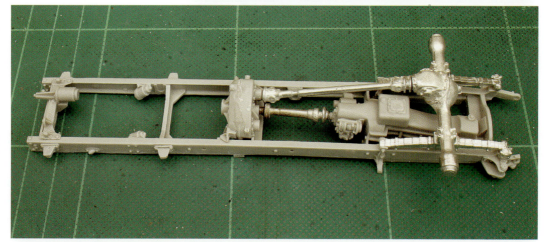

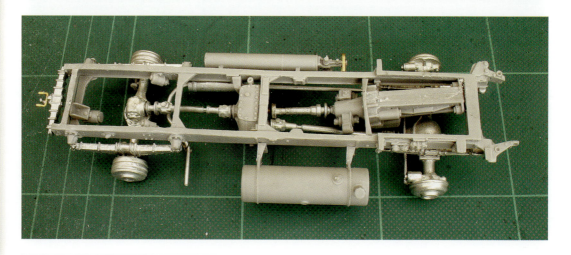

Here's the underside of the gun showing where some parts go.

This is where the instrument panel and fire extinguisher go inside the cab.

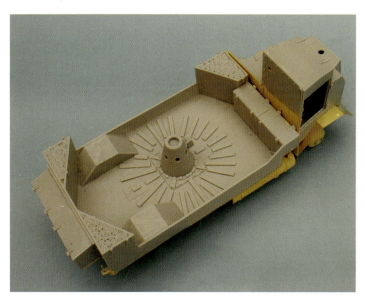

The cab and body are now in place. Both of them need to have some areas painted before fixing because you can't reach them to paint afterwards although they're visible.

BELOW The cab must be pushed right down so its supports meet the chassis and the cab itself sits on the mudguards properly.

them with gentle heat as already described. If the chassis has several parts you will need to build it on a flat surface and keep checking that you are building it flat and straight.

Now add the springs and axles. Some kits have rather vague locating points, so hold the body and cab onto the chassis and make sure the axles will be centred under the mudguards. You will sometimes find that axles are not on the centres of their springs, because many vehicles had springs that were longer in front of the axle than behind. Make sure your springs are the right way round by checking with the instruction sheet's illustrations! It's important to get solid joints for these parts so always use two-part epoxy glue here. Look at how the drive shafts run before you add the axles; you usually need to add each one at the same time as its axle. Build double rear axles together on a flat surface like a small separate chassis. Having individual springs and axles does mean that you may find one or two wheels not touching the ground. If you find this problem just use your knife blade to break the seal of the glue on whichever axle is causing the problem and put a thin scrap of card on its mounts as a spacer before reattaching it.

The engine comes next and in the Deacon it isn't straight, so dry-fit the engine and the cab so you can see how it should fit before you glue it. If it still turns out to be not quite right when you fix the cab just trim a little resin from wherever it obstructs the fit.

When you fix the wheels onto the axles look for a flat place on their tyres. Some kits, like this Deacon, provide this to reproduce the slight bulge of a tyre bearing weight, and of course it has to go on the bottom. If there isn't a flat place put the point where the tyre was attached to its casting plug at the bottom and hide the place that you had to clean up. Plastic kits of wheeled vehicles often come with soft rubber-like tyres, and these usually have moulding seams that are very hard to cut away with a knife blade. I use cuticle trimmers instead. They have small, sharp, angled cutters and make the job of removing tyre seams very easy, just nibble away a bit at a time and work around the tyre.

The finished Deacon.

A SIMPLE SCRATCH-BUILT CONVERSION

Scratch-building is the term we use to talk about making our own parts. It is rare to find a completely scratch-built model, because nearly all of them use kit parts like wheels or tracks. Those who can and do make everything for themselves are the real expert modellers, who usually make one wheel or a track link and then cast as many resin copies as they need for the model.

Here I'm going to show you how to use basic scratch-building methods to turn the Tamiya M3A2 US half-track into the M2. Tamiya's kit represents the final version of the M3 troop carrier, with a 'pulpit' for its machine gun over the cab area and seating for 11 men in the back. The M2 had a shorter body arranged for seven men beside large stowage lockers. The M2 and M3 half-tracks had skid rails around the inside tops of their bodies for machine guns on movable mounts that could slide along. The A1 replaced the skid rail with the 'pulpit', and the final A2 for the M3 had further improvements. Turning the M3A2 into an M2 means making a new rear body, internal rearrangements including stowage lockers, and adding the skid rail, but the chassis, cab and engine area remained the same. I used aftermarket items to upgrade the wheels and tracks and to open the engine compartment, but you don't have to. Tamiya makes other M3 versions but this is the best one to use because the floors of the others need more work.

FIRST, LOOK TO SEE WHAT YOU NEED TO DO

The first thing to do for a scratch-build is plan it. Analyse the kit that parts will come from to see what can be used and what must be made by you, or analyse scale plans and photographs to see what you can find in kits for your scratch-built hull or chassis.

I used a scale plan by George Bradford, reproduced here with his permission. He has many other plans, listed on his AFV News website. I also used photographs in several books, particularly *Half-Track, A History of American Semi-Tracked Vehicles*, by R. P. Hunnicutt,

ITEMS USED

Tamiya M3A2 Half-track (35070)

Plus Model set 151, US Troop Carrier Half-track engine set (White 160AX engine)

R&J resin front wheels and tracks (35206)

K59 resin idler and sprocket set, M3 wheel set (C-002)

Eduard etched-brass set 35447 for M3A2 Half-track

Eduard etched-brass set 3537 US floor plate

Formations US Sherman tool set

Decalcomaniacs US National Insignia 1940-42 (DM-016)

Decalcomaniacs US Light Tanks 1920-42 marking (DM-015)

Polystyrene sheet, 5-, 10-, 20- and 40-thou

Polystyrene rod, pack of assorted sizes

Polystyrene strip, pack of assorted sizes

Fine lead substitute fisherman's fly-tying wire

ABOVE One of the Tamiya base kit options. Tamiya has three US half-track kits, all quite old but re-released regularly. This is the easiest one to use for this conversion because its body floor is simple to adapt.

BELOW The Eduard M3A2 half-track etched set has a lot of parts that are useful for this conversion.

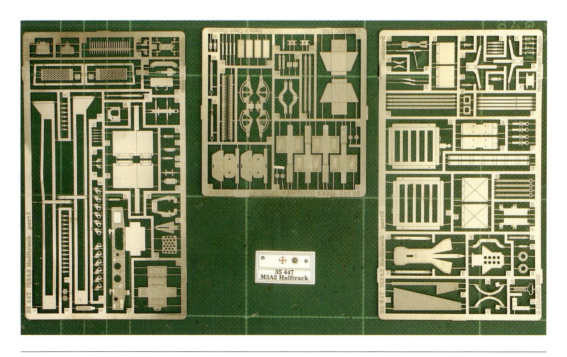

Chapter 7 • A simple scratch-built conversion

M2 Half-track Car

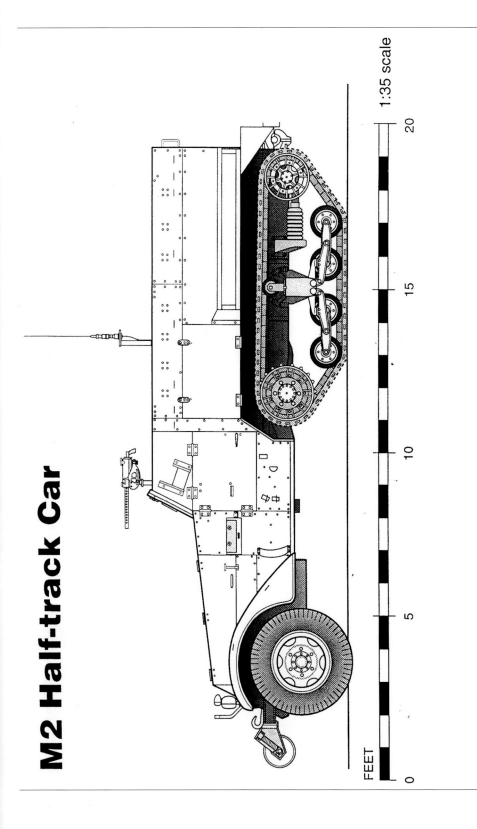

This 1/35-scale plan of the M2 half-track shows what you need to know to carry out the conversion described here. It is reproduced by permission from George Bradford's range of plans. By comparing it with Tamiya's M3A2 half-track kit you can see that the chassis and rear body are shorter and the internal arrangement is different, but this is a simple first conversion because the engine bay and cab are the same as the kit.

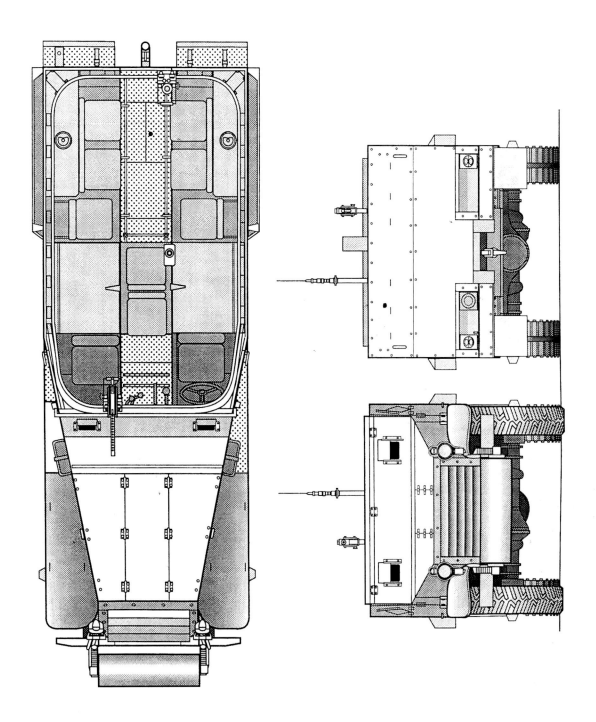

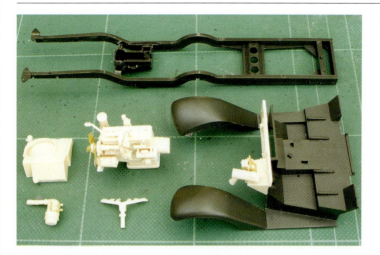

The engine subassemblies and the modified chassis and cab floor.

This is how the engine and firewall fit to the chassis and cab.

The sump protector supports fit like this.

Cut off the back of the chassis at this point and add the rear suspension.

The chassis is now complete so you can start work on the body.

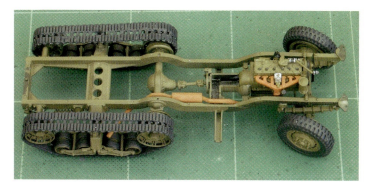

Cut the back of the floor away here and separate the fuel tanks for repositioning.

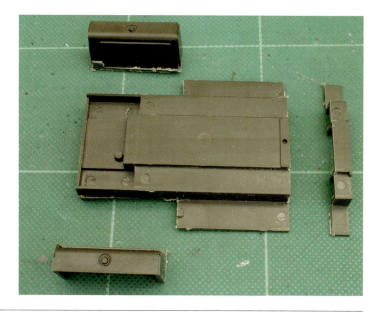

which your local library should be able to get for you. This has the most photographs of the version I wanted to build, but the Osprey *New Vanguard 11: M3 Infantry Half-Track 1940–73* by Steven J. Zaloga, is good too and is cheap enough for you to buy your own copy.

Armed with these I could sort out what I needed to do. The chassis, cab and engine bonnet needed no alteration so the main work was going to be the rear body. This meant changes to Tamiya's floor because it included the M3 seats and was too long for an M2. Because I wanted to fit an aftermarket engine I also had to cut away part of Tamiya's, and this needed to come first because everything else would be built onto the chassis.

STARTING THE WORK

I started by buying the Verlinden engine set, but discarded it after checking it against photographs of the real engine and bought the Plus Models set to use instead. This goes together well and is a good replica of the real thing. Its instructions are good, showing you exactly what has to be done. With the engine built and ready to paint you can move on to the chassis, and all you need to do is cut its end away behind the last cross-member to match the plan's length.

There's no support point on the chassis where the cab and body

floors meet so you must cement them solid to make a single unit. Then you can dry-fit it to the chassis and see where to cut off its end, right over the end of the chassis. You also need to cut away the two fuel tanks without damaging them; they are going to be reused. Clean them up so their sides and ends are smooth and put them aside for later.

Now it's time to add the suspension. R&J Enterprises' M3 wheel set gives resin front wheels and tracks to go on the back and also includes K59's resin idlers and sprockets, which are a vast improvement over Tamiya's. K59 had already donated an idler and sprocket set so I had spares in case of accident. In fact they were very easy to assemble and use so the spares weren't needed. Tamiya's front suspension is used straight from the box, but its axles need to be shortened a little to let the wheels fit properly. The rear suspension is also straight from the box except for K59's idlers and sprockets, and R&J's tracks just slip into place. Now paint the chassis and fit the engine and exhaust pipe.

BEGINNING THE SCRATCH-BUILT PARTS

Now fill in where the fuel tanks were removed, with 40-thou plastic card to match the thickness of the original plastic. Card thickness (and rod diameter) is usually

measured in thousands of an inch (usually expressed as 'thou'). Thus 40-thou is 40 thousandths, or 1mm, while 20-thou is 0.5mm and 10-thou is 0.25mm. Use a pencil and your steel ruler to draw lines where you need to cut, and 'measure twice, cut once'. Cut pieces roughly 10mm wide and 33mm long and cement them solidly to the floor unit (the exact size depends on where you cut the floor), filling the joints afterwards and trimming where needed to get a straight edge all along the outside of the floor. Use your saw, not a knife, to cut 40-thou card and then your file to clean up the edge. Thinner card can be cut with your knife. Cutting card often leaves a raised edge on one or both sides of the card. You will need your file to remove this so there's a flat surface.

Now you need a new body rear plate. Cut 20-thou card 54mm wide and 30mm high, and cut from its lower corners oblongs 10mm wide and 7mm high. Make sure these will fit flush with the ends of the track recesses under the floor and that the full-width section overlaps each edge of the floor unit by 0.5mm. Always cut a little oversize and trim to fit correctly. Now scribe a line between the tops of those cut-outs and another one from side to side 12mm from the top edge – these are plate separation lines on the real M2. To scribe a line simply draw it with your pencil and ruler

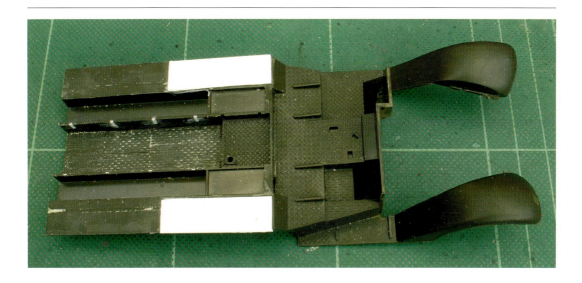

and then, with your ruler against the line as a guide, run the back of your knife's tip along it once or twice. You don't want to cut through, just to have a line visible in the card. Special scribing tools are available, and it is worth getting one, but you can do the job just as well like this. Look at the line closely and you'll see that 'raised edge' again as a tiny, partly detached strip of plastic – run your knife along it to peel it away.

Rivets, love them or hate them they have to be shown

These bodies were riveted, so you need to make rivets. The traditional way is to use a punch and die set to punch dozens of little rivets from 5-thou plastic card and cement them in place. This is time-consuming, boring and leaves little ring-like marks of liquid cement around each rivet. Instead I used a new tool made by Brach Models and available from Italian Kits that punches partway through the plastic from the back and leaves a nice domed rivet on the outside. It comes as a set of four sizes for different-sized rivets or different thicknesses of card, and all you do is push the tip of the tool into the card.

So the next things needed are positions for the rivets. Draw pencil lines down the inside of the plate 0.5mm in from each side, and lines across 0.5mm above and below the tops of the cut-outs and 9.5 and 10.5mm from the top of the plate. On the two 'side' lines mark positions 0.5mm from the top and bottom. Then mark the points where the two 'central' lines cross these, and centrally between each of those and the top and bottom positions. Mark more positions on the two lines placed

ABOVE Use 40-thou card to fill the spaces where the fuel tanks originally were, and remove the locating ribs and the floor plate detail.

BELOW Eduard's etched US anti-slip plate. Other makers also offer this pattern.

between the cut-outs, on the 'central' lines, at 7.5mm spaces and 0.5mm above the bottom lined up below these. You need rivets for the supports of the skid rail, too, so draw lines across the plate 3 and 4.5mm from its top and mark rivet positions on them 2, 10, 11.5, 17 and 18.5mm from each side. That's the marking complete, so push the tool's tip into each marked place and the rivets are done. This sounds like a lot of work, but it took me longer to type than it did to do the work. If you prefer to use the punch and die method the rivet positions are exactly the same but your marks will be on the outside of the plate.

Complete the cab next

Now build the cab, including the panels around the engine, but first cut along the lines on the bonnet where its sides hinge up, leaving the centre strip. This leaves you with the central part so you can get the radiator armour lined up. Cut the bonnet sides away at their hinge line too. Then add the interior etched parts, fix the sides and bonnet top and paint under the whole floor, and then cement it to the chassis. The interior is olive drab, and so are the seat cushions and backs though they were fabric, not paint, and varied in shade. Add a bit of earth brown to your olive drab paint for some seat parts, and a bit of buff or pale sand to it for others, and mix the two results for yet others so you get this variation in colour.

Now for the sides

The body sides need to extend from the back of the cab to the body rear with the rear plate overlapping them, which is why you made the rear plate extend 0.5mm beyond the floor. They need to be 23mm high and about 70mm long. Measure across the floor between the cab sides and cut a piece of sprue to that length, then fix it temporarily between the tops of the sides to keep them vertical. Now measure along the floor and also measure the distance from the top of the cab to the rear plate with that plate held vertical, and you have your measurements for the sides.

They need rows of rivets too, but now you know how to mark the rivet spacing for the rear plate you're able to work out those for the side plates yourself by referring to the plan. Make a note of the measurements of the stowage locker openings and scribe lines on the outsides of the side plates to represent them. Don't lose the note, you'll need it later. When you are satisfied with your rivets and locker openings (never be reluctant to throw a part out and start again if you find you've got it wrong) cement the sides and rear plate in place.

Now you can detail the inside of the body. Take your measurements from the plan and double-check them against your model, just in case your body is a fraction longer or wider than the plan.

Start with the floor. The anti-slip plates on it are laid to a different pattern than the kit's, so cut new ones from an etched set. Several makers produce this pattern. A short single plate is at the back, with a split section in front of it and two large single plates in front of those. They should reach the line between the stowage lockers that you scribed on the side plates. The next section is level with the side floors so cut a strip of card to fit across the floor and add a flat plate (not anti-slip) to make the raised area. Now make the lockers either side, taking their height from the note you made of the size of their doors outside and their other dimensions from the plan. Add a length of thin plastic rod 3.5mm in from the outside to represent the piano hinge used for their lids, and make simple hasp-

Here are front and side views of a machine-gun skid, plus one in its three component parts.

TOP I used the Mission Models Grab Handler with soft-metal fly-tying wire to make all the tie-downs for this model.

BOTTOM The result should look like this.

type fasteners to hold the lids down – the working parts aren't shown on the plan, but they're the same size as the tops that you can see. With the lockers in place you can take away the temporary brace between the cab sides. Next are the foot rails along the sides, and Eduard provides their supports so all you have to do is superglue those in place and slip lengths of plastic rod through them.

Now you can put the fuel tanks at the rear of the body, and work on the seats. Tamiya's seat backs work well for those on the fuel tanks, but you'll need to make new cushions, shown in many photographs as squashed after hard use. Cut squares of 20-thou card to match the cushion sizes on the plan, then press epoxy putty into squarish shapes over these – your fingers will leave suitable squashed centres, but use a drop of water to smooth out your fingerprints. The M2 has three extra seats in the back, so cut three card backs to match Tamiya's part B24 and use the same method to give them well-used pads. Two of them go on card strips cut to match their height and bring them out from the sides as the plan shows; the third needs more work because it had a folding back so I made one of mine folded down. Use plastic rod bent to the shape of the Tamiya item and fixed to the back of the pad, or show both your seats erect so their backs hide any problems you have in making the supports.

To finish the interior bodywork you need some plastic strip 3mm wide. Cut lengths to fit between the stowage bins and the fuel tanks, and across the rear plate, at the height of the centre line you scribed on that earlier. Put 'rivets' on them to correspond with the ones outside, and cement them in place. The bottom of the rear plate, where it meets the floor, gets a 1.5mm strip with rivets and at seat height there's another one with a 1mm strip added on top to make an L shape.

THE SKID RAIL AND MACHINE GUNS

The skid rail is awkward to make because it has to bend round four corners, as well as up at the front. Try to find some brass I-beam in a model railway shop, 3mm deep and 1.5mm across its top. Bend it to follow the shape you can see on the plan and on my model, starting at the centre of the rear plate and working round till the other end meets it. Then saw off the excess and cut pieces of 40-thou card to superglue inside it where the squares of rivets are on the sides and rear plate. The front support is another piece of 40-thou card cut to the shape of the rail, and all the supports should keep the rail just clear of the body sides. I had to use Plastruct I-beam, not nearly so easy to bend to shape because it splits if put under too much stress, but if you bend it gently, a little at a time instead of trying to make a complete bend all at once, it can be persuaded into the right shape. I made my skid rail in two parts, left and right, to avoid trying to make a complete rail in one piece and having it break at the last bend. Whether brass or plastic, joints can be hidden by putting the machine-gun mounts over them.

I've included a photograph to show the shape of those mounts because it is a peculiar one to make. Use 20-thou card and start with a square the height of the skid rail. On top of this cement a piece with a square the same size projecting over its front and a triangular projection at its back – rather like the end of a marquee to look at, with vertical sides and a pointed roof. A simple square goes at the bottom of the first piece, and the two 'square' sections should fit neatly onto the rail and come a little way beyond it. Now cut a piece of 1mm plastic rod to fit down the first square under that triangular projection. Each side of this gets a small bit of 0.5mm rod as the mounts for the locking handle that stopped the mount sliding. This is two L-shaped pieces cut from card with a length of 1mm rod between their bottom ends. To finish it off you need the

This view into the body shows the rearranged seats and other changes.

handle that was used to slide the mount, and this is simply two short pieces of card at a 45-degree angle on the right-hand side with 1mm rod between them. You need three mounts like this.

Use Tamiya's machine guns, but improve them with Eduard's cradles and barrel jackets. Slice the plastic cradles away carefully and fold the etched ones to shape, then superglue the guns into them after you've dealt with the barrel jackets. The etch is thin enough to roll into shape just by rolling the end of the Multi Tool back and forth over it. Cut off the barrels of the .30-cal. guns and drill a hole for a plastic rod replacement with the length of the jacket left sticking out, then paint it and slip the jacket over it. Drill a hole into the end of the discarded barrel and cut off the end 1mm, then superglue this onto the end of the jacket. The .50-cal. gun is a little trickier – you need to remove the 'perforated' bit by slicing it down to the diameter of the barrel without cutting off the barrel itself – but not hard to do. Complete the guns and superglue them to the sliding mounts at whatever angles you choose; I have the one over the driver's head turned backwards.

SOME EXTRA DETAILS OUTSIDE

You need to fit the tools; either those nice ones from Formations or you can adapt Tamiya's, the

jerrycans in their racks and the folded bonnet and radiator cover. Then you need a line of tie-downs around the body, shown by short lines on the plan and visible on my model. Many etched sets provide these for you as parts to fold to shape, but they are rather 'flat' when you look at them afterwards so here's how to make better ones with a Grab Handler. Get some fly-tying wire from an anglers' shop and cut short lengths. Put one into the jaws of the Grab Handler and bend each side down with your pliers – if you hold the wire about .75mm from the Grab Handler and just press down you will have 'legs' with 'feet' at right angles to them. Cut the feet to 1mm long and squeeze them with your pliers, and they will round out into the exact shape of the real thing's feet. Some will go wrong, this is inevitable, but they're so quick and easy to make that you will very soon have enough good ones for the model.

While you have the Grab Handler out, make two 3mm-long grab handles for the back of the body out of brass rod or copper wire. Just put it into the Grab Handler, bend down each side, cut the legs to 1mm, and superglue them in place.

Finally, you need the rear trackguards. Cut two triangles of 20-thou card to match the plan, one for each side of the body, and oblongs to match the top view. Cover the tops with anti-slip plate,

then cut shapes from 20-thou card to angle down inside the triangular parts – they'll need cut-outs to fit around the body because they go underneath it. Use a piece of paper to work out the shape, cutting it oversize and trimming until it fits, then copying it in card. The inside ends of the top are supported above these by strips of 20-thou card 1mm wide, cut to fit. Across the bottoms go strips of 20-thou card 3mm wide, with 1mm strips of 10-thou card at their tops and bottoms. Cut the taillights from Tamiya's rear plate and cement them into the outer corners, and add a 3mm square of 10-thou card with a 2mm disc in its centre as the electrical connection point for a trailer. Now cement the trackguards into place and the building is finished!

I used a different painting technique for this model, which I built as it would have been in service in Tunisia in 1943. Olive drab overall was the standard finish but I deliberately left it incompletely stirred so it would vary slightly on the model. The painting was done with a brush used up and down, so I got vertical streaks – Tunisia is not a desert area so rain streaks would have shown. The standard markings for this period were yellow stars, one at the rear and one on top of the bonnet, which I took from the Decalcomaniacs range together with the blue serial numbers for an M2.

Hotchkiss Geschützwagen
By Steve Zaloga

On D-Day, Panzergrenadier Regiment 125 counterattacked the British paratroopers of the 6th Airborne Division near Escoville. They were supported by several 10.5cm leFH 18 auf Geschützwagen 38H (f), at least two of which were knocked out. This incident was the inspiration for this model.

A British para calls a halt to his patrol while kneeling next to an abandoned 10.5cm Geschützwagen in Normandy on D-Day.

Items used

Trumpeter German 39(H) 10.5cm Le FH 18(Sf) auf Geschützwagen (00353)
Blast Models update set for 105mm LeFH 18 (sF) auf Geschützwagen 38H(f) (BL35066K)
Ultimate Scenery stone retaining wall
AFV Club German 10.5 howitzer ammunition leFH 18 and accessory set (AF 35062)
Resicast Airborne soldier '…stop…' (35.542)
Friulmodel Hotchkiss track (ATL-68)
Aber nets and drilled plates (S03)

A rear view of the completed model showing the details of the ammunition stowage.

THE SUSPENSION

I started out the project in my usual fashion by tackling the suspension. I made a few modest improvements here such as replacing the solid kit springs with new ones made from wire. I decided to use an aftermarket individual-link track set since the kit tracks are nothing special and the Hotchkiss tended to have pronounced track sag. I used a set of Friulmodel white-metal tracks, courtesy of Bill Miley of Chesapeake Model Designs. My original plan had been to leave the track off the model until after painting, but during the assembly process I became concerned about whether this would be possible as there is very little clearance between the drive sprocket and idler and the fenders. So I decided to attach the

The Hotchkiss Geschützwagen was one of a menagerie of odd conversions carried out under the direction of an artillery officer of the 21st Panzer Division, Major Alfred Becker. Somewhere between 24 and 48 were built so it's surprising that there are already two 1/35-scale kits of the Geschützwagen from Gunze Sanyo and Trumpeter with a third expected from Bronco. The Trumpeter kit used here is a very nice model, though the small details fall a bit short of current standards. I was tempted to tackle this model after seeing the excellent Blast resin upgrade set which brings it up to state-of-the-art standards with many finely detailed substitutes for some of the kit's clunkier parts. There are a number of other upgrade kits available, including several etched-metal sets, but I didn't really feel they were necessary. The aim of this chapter is to provide a brief summary of the construction of this model with a special focus on the special techniques used to enhance the detail, methods to create simple scenic bases and basic approaches to painting figures with acrylics.

An easy way to make new springs for the model is to wrap 20-thou copper wire around a screw of suitable diameter and pitch.

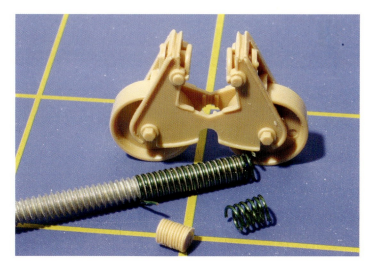

The location of the drive sprocket hole should be moved to the centre. This view also shows the reshaping of the top of the suspension bogies to the proper 'U' cross-section.

track to the suspension before proceeding to the upper hull. I used five-minute epoxy glue to attach the track in place, as I have found that leaving the track loose causes problems with painting and also can lead to the track breaking at inopportune moments.

THE SUPERSTRUCTURE

When building an open-topped armoured vehicle, it's necessary to give some thought to painting since some elements of the interior will be inaccessible or difficult to reach once assembly is complete. As a result, I changed the assembly sequence from that suggested in the kit instructions, for example attaching the fenders earlier in the process. I also added the upper bow plate (part G6) out of sequence since it's necessary to fair this into the rest of the bow casting. This whole bow should appear to be a pair of castings, so after filling the gaps around the drive housings (parts A19–20) and lower hull with putty, I painted the surfaces with some Mr Surfacer 500 and stippled the finish to give it a more uniform cast effect.

Before painting the interior, I had to try to determine the colours. There is only one interior photo of the Geschützwagen from the period, which is printed in the Jentz book (see page 124). My guess from this photo is that the interior had been completed in panzer grey before the new 1943 dark yellow regulations took effect, and that interior components added later such as the gun assembly and engine deck were finished in dark yellow like the exterior of the vehicle.

Although there are aftermarket etched-metal sets to replace the superstructure in brass, I had little interest in rebuilding the entire superstructure to make the armoured walls appear thinner.

Trumpeter does a credible job to achieve this effect by creating a 'knife-edge' effect near the top of the superstructure, gradually blending the kit parts from the usual 40-thou thickness to a more realistic 10-thou thickness. I amplified this effect with some careful sanding and file work, so that the blend line between the thick and thin parts of the panel were less obvious and I thinned the upper edge of the plates. Once the dark grey paint is applied, the thickness of the plates looks quite convincing.

With the superstructure panels prepared, I decided to assemble the whole upper superstructure to make certain that it all fitted properly. While the kit instructions recommend attaching all the interior detail prior to assembling the basic components, I don't like having a lot of delicate parts in place in the event that there are fit problems. After fitting the basic superstructure together I attempted to fit it to the lower hull. I found that it did not fit properly, with the assembly being about 2mm too far to the rear, which left a gap in the upper bow plate and the driver's plate. The culprit seemed to be the joint between the engine firewall in the lower hull (part A6)

The Blast resin interior is a substantial upgrade to the kit details.

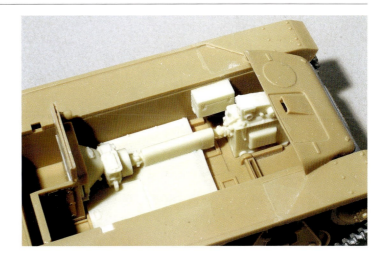

The superstructure interior is ready for the airbrush, but some items have been left off for ease of painting.

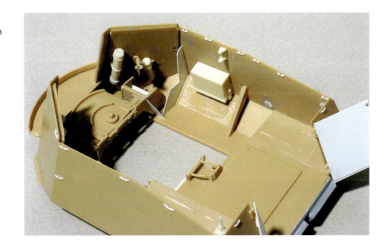

The interior of the superstructure includes a mixture of kit parts, Blast resin upgrades, and small detail additions such as the wiring for the FuG 5 radio.

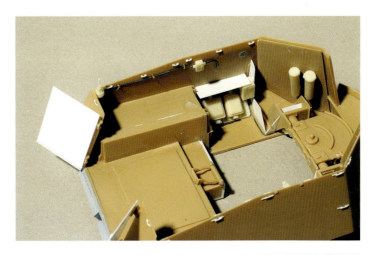

Disposable plastic cards make a good painting platform when airbrushing small components. Each of these cards is separated by the different colour to be used. Cross-action tweezers are good for delicate parts or single items.

After the interior was painted, the engine deck was masked off, dampened with water, and sprinkled with salt to create a mask.

The engine deck was sprayed the yellow exterior colour and then the salt brushed off to reveal this chipped finish.

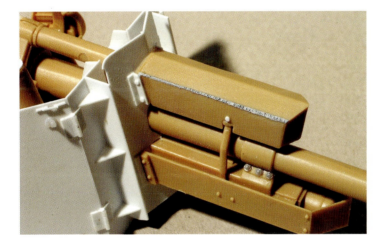

TOP Weld beads on the recuperator cover were created by masking the area and then painting on a thin bead of Tamiya putty.

BOTTOM Putty weld beads are a good way to simulate the real thing since they can be sanded if the original attempt is too prominent.

and the left-side projection on the superstructure rear floor (part F26). To fix the problem, I sawed off the front face of the panel on F26, which is hidden by the other part.

Although the basic kit superstructure parts had reasonably thin edges after modification, some of the other kit parts would be more difficult to thin to a convincing degree. This is particularly the case of the rear doors (parts E4, E5), the forward armoured shield around the howitzer (parts, F2, F3, F27 and G45) and the internal bracing (parts F21, F32). I decided to replace these all with sheet plastic. I would not necessarily recommend this project to less experienced modellers; in particular the front shield assembly requires a bit of skill to recreate in sheet plastic. However, most modellers with a minimum of practice with sheet plastic should be able to manage to duplicate the rear doors and the internal braces. I used a mixture of 10- and 15-thou sheet plastic for these parts. On some other parts, for example the armoured shield around the howitzer frame (parts G37, G38, G39), I used the 'knife-edge' trick to thin the upper edges to make them appear closer to scale thickness.

DETAILING THE MODEL

The interior leaves open a lot of room for detail work, though the Blast kit provides most of the necessary components. I added some wiring detail around the FuG 5 radio based on the Blast instruction sheet and colour photos in Pierre Metsu's *Les Materiels radio de la Wehrmacht 1935–1945* (Heimdal, 2004). The rest of the interior came either from kit parts or the Blast substitutes. I attached some parts directly to the superstructure walls prior to painting, but left off a good many assemblies such as the ammunition bins, flag rack and other items that would be difficult or impossible to paint if attached.

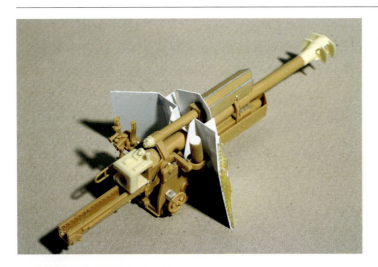

The kit's armoured shield at the front of the gun was replaced by sheet plastic while the breech and muzzle brake came from the Blast set.

The Geschützwagen had some wire screens attached to the front of the armour shield for attaching foliage camouflage, done here using Aber photo-etch.

The Blast set provided some more delicate details for items such as the muffler and engine exhaust gratings.

The bow was painted with Mr Surfacer to give a cast texture, while a weld bead was added to the curved panel over the driver's hatch using a piece of 10-thou plastic rod soaked in liquid cement to give it a more uneven texture. Other points worth noting are the plastic sheet reinforcements on the forward bogie and the small tools and fitting added from the excellent Blast resin upgrade kit.

A left front view of the completed model prior to painting. As can be seen, the finished model is something of a mixed media project with resin, sheet plastic, photo-etch and white metal. This also necessitated the usual mixture of glues, including Tamiya liquid plastic cement, cyranoacrylate glue and five-minute epoxy.

A left rear view of the completed model prior to painting. This rear view accents the decision to paint the interior before proceeding to the exterior finish. I prefer to paint as much of the model as possible together to obtain uniformity, but on complicated vehicles such as this one, preliminary painting of the interior is almost inevitable. Notice that some of the interior parts are not attached at this stage to ease the masking process.

A right front view of the completed model prior to painting. This view accents the large amount of flat surface on the superstructure that has the potential to be very boring unless some interesting camouflage and weathering is applied. Fortunately, the Normandy schemes were just the right solution for this dilemma.

A right rear view of the completed model prior to painting. A few of the items left off the model before final painting were the resin ammunition stowage bins, as they would simply make it more difficult to mask the rear compartment. Some of the more delicate items were left off as well.

The model prepared for painting with the interior masked off and the separate components mounted on painting cards. The edges of the fighting compartment were lined with the wide Tamiya yellow 'kabuki' masking tape which is thin, flexible and not too adhesive. The interior of the vehicle was stuffed with tissue to fill the large volume. Blue painter's tape was used to hold the tissue in place, as it is tackier and more economical than specialized hobby tape.

Aside from using the Blast breech and muzzle brake assemblies, I made few other changes to the kit howitzer. The elevating wheel on the right side of the gun is mounted too low, and requires a small extension upward so that it will clear the gun mount. The exterior gun-shield was regularly fitted with a piece of wire fencing for attaching camouflage as a factory-fitted item, and I added this to the model using a piece of photo-etched Aber screen. I made a few modest changes on the exterior detail such as some aiming stakes at the rear, a tow cable on the front, stowage eyelets around the superstructure top, and various bits of packing material for 105mm ammunition from the excellent AFV Club set.

Painting the model

Before getting into the precise details of painting, a few words about the equipment I use. I have used an airbrush since I was teenager, so I cannot fathom why serious modellers would not use one as it is much easier than hand painting once the basic techniques are learned. Over the years I've gotten better equipment than my original 1960s Binks airbrush and Sears compressor, but this was partly due to the fact that I acquired some of it to do technical artwork in the 1980s that required more precise equipment. My compressor is a German Art International with a holding tank, pressure regulator and water trap. This was a major investment when I bought it 20 years ago for about $350 on sale at a local art store. For an airbrush, I use a Badger 100G with a fine tip for about 99 per cent of my work. Most modellers seem to prefer airbrushes with side or bottom-fed cups which I absolutely detest since they are such a nuisance to clean. I prefer a simple gravity-feed airbrush because it is very simple to clean between colours using Q-tip cotton swabs and Windex household cleaner. A minor drawback is that the cup is rather small, so I may have to refill it twice during an average painting session.

I also have an Iwata CM-B, which has the same configuration as the Badger, but is more finely machined and has a screw adjuster to limit how far the trigger can be pulled back to limit the size of the spray. By way of cost comparison, I recently replaced my ten-year-old Badger with a new one for under $60 while the Iwata cost me about $350 when I bought it 20 years ago to do artwork. The Iwata is very helpful when doing very fine patterns such as the camouflage on this model, but I don't regularly use it since I tend to do US vehicles that have simpler finishes. I would only recommend a high-end brush like the Iwata to people who want to do very intricate hand-applied paint schemes. A Badger in good condition can do most work, including a lot of fine painting, so long as the tip and pin are in good shape and the airbrush is kept clean.

I only airbrush with acrylics with the exception of the final application of flat finish where I use Testors' lacquer-based Dullcote

My workhorse airbrush is the Badger 100G, a gravity-fed, double-action, internal mix type with a fine tip.

due to its application over a mixed acrylic/oil-wash finish. I use acrylics for a few reasons. They are far less toxic than enamels and their solvents, and they are much more forgiving if a mistake is made since they can be cleaned off the plastic model with little effort. I primarily use Tamiya acrylics as I have found them to be of high quality with good coating and consistent performance. I don't like many of the other acrylics on the market as they behave somewhat like acrylic house-paint. They tend to develop a thin 'skin' while drying, which leads to excessive paint jams in my airbrush. On the other hand, Tamiya is not suitable for hand painting and instead I use Vallejo, Vallejo Game and Andrea acrylics for brush painting.

Modellers tend to fall into one of two categories of painting style – artists or engineers. The engineers insist on matching each colour exactly to the original colour standards. Artists use the original colour standards as a basis, but try to make the model look like a miniature example of the full-scale vehicle. I fall into the 'artist' category as I find that matching the colours precisely results in a model that appears to be far too dark. So I start with a colour that is close to the original full-scale colour, and then lighten it in an effort to result in a small-scale colour. Another point to keep in mind before applying paint is

the effect of any washes that will be applied. I try to compensate for this in advance, keeping the original colour a bit lighter if I plan to apply any dark washes.

On this model I used Tamiya XF-22 RLM Grey rather than XF-63 German Grey as the interior colour, both for scale affect and to compensate for the sepia wash I intended to apply over it. I used the 'salt mask' approach to depict the scuffing and chipping that would occur on engine deck plate that would have suffered heavy abuse. After the base grey was dry, I dampened the surface with water using my airbrush and then drizzled on a mixture of kosher and sea salt. Once the water had evaporated, I sprayed this area with my dark yellow mixture, and once dry, I brushed away the salt. This leaves a nice, beat-up finish that is hard to duplicate using a brush.

The lower hull was airbrushed in Tamiya XF-72 JSDF brown as the basic dirt colour. My aim was to depict a vehicle moving over moist soil where the soil colour covered everything including the contact surfaces of the wheels and tracks. The upper surfaces were then airbrushed in a lightened dark yellow, which was roughly half XF-60 Dark Yellow and half white. To simulate the natural effect of weathering and rain wash on the superstructure, I used my Iwata to apply a streaked pattern on the vertical surfaces, and a more

irregular pattern on the other surfaces, with the airbrush set at a very fine pattern and the pressure cranked way down. I used two colours for this, lighter and darker versions of the dark yellow I had already applied. On the undersides, I sprayed some irregular patterns over the starting brown, with Tamiya XF-57 Buff and then highlighting this on the more exposed surfaces with buff substantially lightened with white to suggest dried dirt.

Once the basic colours were on, I then applied the camouflage colours. I used Tamiya XF-73 Dark Green for the 'scale-effect' green and I mixed up my own dark brown. I applied these with my Iwata at low pressure, and used a photo in the Spielberger book (see page 124) as a general guide to the pattern. I then blended together the dirt-covered bottom areas with the cleaner upper surfaces by lightly spraying some buff and lightened buff over the dividing area to suggest dust and dried earth. Once the basic airbrushing was done, I then did a little chipping and scuffing. This is the current fad among 'extreme' modellers, especially among German AFV modellers. I think it is often overdone, but it is a worthwhile effect if done in a subtle fashion. I did some chipping in the interior with a brush and thinned dark grey paint, but on the exterior, I mainly used a dark

The first stage of airbrushing covered the upper surfaces with dark yellow and the undersides with a suitable dark earth colour.

The second stage of painting began the weathering process by streaking the dark sections with lighter and darker shades of the colour, and adding colour depth to the dirty area with additional dry earth colours.

The two camouflage colours were added next with a fine Iwata airbrush set at low pressure and then the upper and lower colours were blended by light oversprays of dusty colours.

The final paint scheme added chipping as well as a glaze to simulate dust and mute the contrast of the camouflage colours.

This close-up shows the fine chipping done with a colour pencil.

The wash, chipping and highlighting serve to accent fine detail such as on the recuperator cover.

ABOVE The finished model before the foliage was added from the right front.

LEFT The finished model from the left front with the foliage in place The foliage adds a lot of interest to the model, giving it a different texture and colour. The use of sea-foam weed with attached leaves is one of the simplest and most effective methods to depict foliage in this scale. Although there are photo-etch alternatives, they are very expensive for such a large volume, and lack the natural 'fractal' appearance of real plant material.

The finished model from the right rear. Self-propelled artillery are one of the most attractive types of AFV models since the open fighting compartment provides a wealth of opportunity for both detail and colour variation as is obvious here. This also requires quite a bit more care in the final finishing process, especially in planning when and how all the separate components will be painted.

The finished model from the left rear. The view from this angle again accents the attractiveness that the foliage adds to the model by breaking up the monotony of the flat exterior panels as well as adding a distinctly different colour. Likewise, the use of two leaf colours breaks up the foliage colour, giving it a more varied appearance.

A view into the right side of the fighting compartment. The ammunition packing crates are from the AFV Club kit. The ammunition packing was deliberately placed in a bit of a jumble both to make the interior more interesting, as well as to suggest that the vehicle might have been abandoned in haste. A model like this offers considerable opportunities for variation in the colour of the interior due to the use of various components with different colours and finishes.

A view of the right side of the fighting compartment. The Blast ammunition racks are a major improvement to the kit, and a tarp has been added over them from lead sheet. Artillery pieces can be made more interesting by all the assorted paraphernalia of the associated ammunition. There are wooden crates for the projectiles, but also there are stowage containers for the propellant bag charges and even fuse containers. This offers even more potential for colour variety since some of the items such as the wooden packing crates were left in their natural wood colour.

TOP LEFT The mixed panzer grey/dark yellow interior fittings add life to the overall scheme.

BOTTOM LEFT The foliage on the Hotchkiss was made from seafoam weed seen in the box to the right with two colours of Noch leaves as seen to the left, attached using 3M spray photo adhesive with a final coat of hairspray for better adhesion.

brown Derwent watercolour pencil sharpened to a fine point. Once all the detail painting was completed, I applied a glaze over the upper surfaces using a 50:50 mixture of Tamiya thinner and clear, which was coloured with a bit of buff. The aim here is to give the surface a slightly smooth surface for applying the weathering wash, but also to mute the contrast in the colours and chipping by simulating the effect of dust.

Once the acrylics were dry, I applied a wash consisting of mineral spirits and Holbein Sepia oil paint. I used more paint on the lower dirty sections of the chassis, and less paint on the upper dark yellow sections. On the vertical surfaces, I applied the wash in vertical streaks to simulate the effects of rain, while I applied it more uniformly on the lower surfaces. After letting the wash dry for a few days, I went back and did some highlighting. I used drybrushing techniques for most of this, starting with an enamel colour close to the area to be highlighted, then lightened with titanium white oil paint for better blending. So on the interior surfaces, I started with some Humbrol Dark Grey, while on the dark yellow surfaces I used a beige shade. After letting everything dry, I applied a coat of Testors' Dullcote with my airbrush to flatten the finish. Once this was dry, I went back for some final effects, such as powdered graphite wiped on the track to simulate wear.

German tanks in Normandy were usually festooned with foliage camouflage to ward off the Allied fighter-bombers. To duplicate this on my Geschützwagen, I started with some seafoam weed that can be obtained from model railway specialists such as Scenic Express in the US under their 'Super-trees' brand. After cutting off some suitable branches, I sprayed the upper portions using 3M photo-adhesive. I then dipped these into a little heap of leaves mixed from Noch Lime leaves (08020 *mittelgrün*) and birch leaves (08010 *hellgrün*). To help fix the leaves on the branches, I then coated them with some hairspray for better adhesion. I then attached these to the model with a little Walther's Goo contact cement to make sure they stayed in place.

THE BASE

I always mount my models on small scenic bases, which serves the dual purpose of establishing the geographic context for the vehicle as well as protecting the model. I usually use an inexpensive photo

frame as the base with a piece of plexiglass (Perspex) on top. I prefer plexiglass over wood or other materials as it is less likely to warp over time. For this model, I decided to depict the vehicle after it was abandoned while travelling down a country lane. On one side is a small stone wall, made from a section of expanded resin foam retaining wall from the Ultimate Scenery line I found at a local railway model shop. The elevated terrain behind it was made with a wedge-shaped box made from 30-thou sheet plastic. The terrain itself was made from Apoxie epoxy putty. I left a relatively clean area where the tracks of the tank would sit, and I masked this area with tape. After mixing up a batch of putty about the size of a golf ball, I spread it out over the plexiglass. I made a distinct hump in the centre of the road as though wheeled traffic has worn it down on either side over time. Once I had roughly covered the surface and removed the tape, I went back over the putty with my finger dampened in rubbing alcohol to smooth it out a bit and remove any fingerprints or irregularities. To give it some more natural texture, I pressed in some small stones from a local model railway shop, and then textured the surface. I began the texturing process using a rough plastic sponge of the type sold in do-it-yourself shops for stripping paint. This gave a good rough texture,

and then I used a stiff stencil brush for some more delicate effects. Once this had dried overnight, I did any cleanup necessary, and then painted it. The soil colours were the same as on the tank model, starting with XF-72 Brown. Once the airbrushing was finished and the paint dry, I did the same sort of wash and dry-brushing as on the tank model to pop out the texture. I then added foliage effects. In this case, the grass areas in the foreground came from a small section of Heki 'wildgras waldboden 1576' while the foliage above the wall was from Silflor Birch Tree Horsetail foliage attached to the base using Walther's Goo contact cement.

THE FIGURE

I find that a well-painted figure considerably enhances the appearance of a tank model since it provides a sense of scale. A secondary, though less appreciated, effect is that it confirms that the modeller is a skilled painter since current styles of extreme weathering can give the impression to the casual viewer that the model is sloppily painted. I chose Resicast's excellent British paratrooper figure with two small changes – I reoriented the head sideways and I reoriented the hand slightly.

I do not have the space here to go into much detail about painting techniques, as that would take a

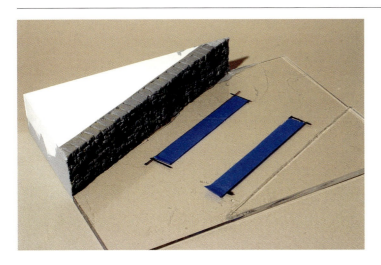

The base begins as a piece of plexiglass with the large architectural elements glued in place, and the mounting area of the Hotchkiss tracks masked off.

The Apoxie Sculpt epoxy putty is applied roughly over the base.

After the epoxy putty is smoothed, texture is added by pressing in some small rocks, using a rough plastic sponge and stencil brush to stipple in additional surface texture.

The earth colours of the base are painted using the same shades as on the model starting with a dark earth colour and followed by lighter shades to simulate dried dirt.

After the airbrushing, the base receives a wash of mineral spirits mixed with sepia oil paint, followed by dry-brushing to pop out the texture.

BELOW The finished model on its base using an inexpensive picture frame found at a local Ikea furniture store.

book in itself. But I can explain some of my approaches. To begin with, dedicated figure painters will spend 40 hours or more on a single figure, about the same time a tank modeller will spend on their tank. I'm not willing to spend that amount of time on a figure, and my figures probably take me 4–5 hours to paint. So I don't use the elaborate styles of highlighting and shading used by some figure modellers. I try for a less time-consuming approach and the montage of six photos here shows my figure as it progressed at roughly 45-minute intervals.

My first admonition is that, unless you are a superior painter, don't even think about trying to paint eyes. I have seen far too many tank models ruined by goofy looking figures with enormous white blobs in their eye-socket. I go for the 'Clint Eastwood stare' – soldiers outdoors in the sun are going to be squinting. To simulate this, I use a sharp pin such as on a pair of dividers, and poke a pair of small holes where the iris should be. It is fairly easy to let a little dark wash flood into this area and around the eyelids.

I have been experimenting with a method of 'accent-washes' for the uniform that starts with a basic colour significantly lighter than the final intended coloru. In this case, I started by airbrushing a basecoat of Tamiya White and Dark Yellow the same as the Geschützwagen colour. I then applied the camouflage colours on the battledress in somewhat lighter and brighter shades than normal. These hand-painted camouflage colours always look much too stark compared to real cloth, so I airbrushed on a glaze of Tamiya clear, thinner and a little dark yellow to mute the contrast. Once this was done, I went ahead with detail painting the rucksack, webbing and other kit in lighter shades than the final colour. Once

Eyes can be added to a figure using a sharp pointed tool like these dividers. This method is much simpler than attempting to paint them using more conventional techniques.

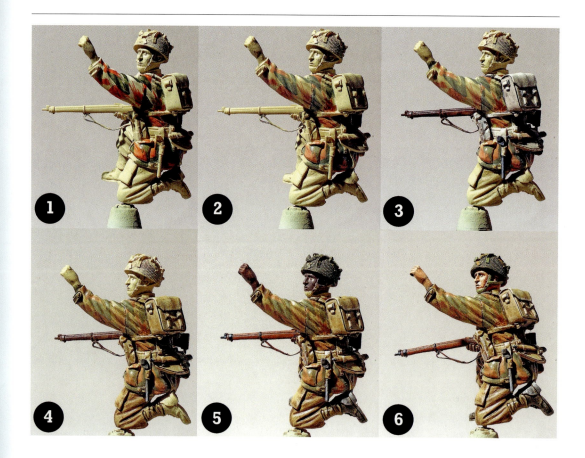

this was done, I applied an accent wash over each of the main colour areas. An accent wash consists of a darker acrylic colour mixed with an acrylic gloss medium and water. It differs from the usual modelling washes in that the gloss medium suspends the paint colour in a fashion different from a solvent such as water. Instead of congregating mostly in the depressions, the medium helps spread the colour over the entire surface, even though it will congregate in the depressions more that on the high points. This is a quick-and-dirty way to simulate traditional highlighting, shading and accenting methods. While it is far from an ideal figure-painting technique, it is better than no effect at all. The accent colour I used on the camouflage uniform was Vallejo 921 English Uniform, while I used a browner shade on the trousers and a lighter shade on the webbing. I usually go back and do some accent painting around the major kit. This is hard to explain in the short space here or even in a longer account, since so much of it depends on the painter's judgement of what needs to be accented.

This montage shows how the Resicast para was painted at roughly 45-minute intervals: 1) base coat and camouflage; 2) glaze to mute and blend the camouflage; 3) detail painting of webbing and kit; 4) applying the accent glazes over the clothing to accentuate the detail and provide a simple highlight/shadowing effect; 5) painting the flesh areas in reverse starting with a dark flesh colour; 6) finishing the flesh areas with a medium and light flesh colour as well as intermediate blending shades.

On this particular figure with the helmet and extensive straps over the face, I decided to paint the flesh colours in reverse starting with a dark brown (Vallejo Game Colour

Some views of the finished Resicast Para figure. While specialist figure painters can no doubt provide a more sophisticated finish, this approach using acrylics results in an attractive figure in a modest amount of time.

45 Charred Brown) then moving on to a deep flesh colour (41 Dwarf Skin) and with the highlights in a light flesh colour (4 Elf Skin). Needless to say, there are a lot of intermediate steps here where I used an intermediate shade to blend the colours, for example, some of the 45 Brown and 41 Dwarf Skin mixed with a little acrylic gloss medium to make blending easier.

There are two critical steps in learning to figure paint. The first is to paint, paint and paint some more. Your first few figures may be grotesque, but you can only gain a painter's eye through experience and frequent practice. The second is to attend shows and read magazines that show figure-painting styles you enjoy. It is easier to decipher how a modeller has painted a figure than to try to copy real life. Have fun!

REFERENCES

Jentz, Tom, and Doyle, Hilary, *Panzer Tracts No. 10: Artillerie Selbstfahrlafetten* (Panzer Tracts: Boyd, MD, 2002)

Militar's Kits 6: Special Normandy (Part 2) (MK Editions: France, 1994)

Panzers at Saumur No. 3 (Model Graphix: Tokyo, 1992)

Spielberger, Walter, *Beute-Kraftfahrzeuge und Panzer der deutchen Wehrmacht* (Motorbuch Verlag: Stuttgart, 1989)

Sturmgeschütz IV

by Gary Edmundson

The following chapter will describe the construction and painting of a 1/35-scale model of the German Panzerjäger Sturmgeschütz IV (StuG IV) used during the last year of World War II. The various techniques used to combine two commercially available kits into one model will be explained, along with guidance on scratch-building the necessary parts to complete the build. The application of *Zimmerit* texture to the kit's surface will also be covered step by step. The section will conclude with combining the finished model with some figures in a realistic vignette setting.

Tamiya's StuG IIIG and Panzer IVJ kits were combined with some aftermarket accessories and scratch-building to produce a 1/35-scale model of the Sturmgeschütz IV.

Items used

Tamiya Panzer IVJ (35181)
Tamiya StuG IIIG Frühe (35197)
Modelkasten Panzer III/IV Track (Type A) (SK-17)
Aber brass fenders for Panzer IV (new style) (35 A81)

PLANNING THE BUILD

Tamiya, Dragon Models Ltd and Italeri produce commercially available kits in 1/35 scale of the StuG IV. The Tamiya and Italeri kits are quite dated, and each has their share of inaccuracies. To construct an accurate model of this vehicle, I decided to combine the later Tamiya version of the StuG IIIG (35197) and Panzer IVJ (35181). Referred to as 'kit-bashing', the upper portion of the StuG III was adapted to the lower hull of the Panzer IV using some key reference drawings from the book *Sturmgeschütz and its Variants* by Walter J. Spielberger.

OPPOSITE PAGE With the kits, reference material and detail parts gathered the modeller is ready to start an ambitious project.

HISTORY

Following the success of the Sturmgeschütz III in its combined role of assault gun and tank hunter, the German high command decided to mount the StuG III superstructure on the Panzer IV chassis in late 1943. This was to make up for lost production at the Alkett factory, which had suffered from heavy bombing. To adapt the StuG III fighting compartment to the Panzer IV chassis, an armoured extension was added at the driver's position, with two periscopes and a small hatch on the roof. The Sturmgeschütz IV went through several minor refinements in a production run from December 1943 to March 1945. A total of 1,139 vehicles were produced, and served with independent StuG brigades belonging to artillery, assault gun detachments, Panzerjäger detachments, and tank detachments of the infantry and Panzer divisions.

The subject of the build was a vehicle photographed at the Krupp factory in September 1944. Since it was manufactured halfway through the production run, the vehicle displayed some earlier and later features of the StuG IV. Since *Zimmerit* anti-magnetic paste was discontinued after September 1944, this would have been one of the last examples to have it applied. The vehicle also had a remotely fired MG34 mount, and the later exhaust pipes with flash suppression. The camouflage scheme applied was soft-edged wavy lines on the vehicle, with side skirts, or *Schürzen*, painted in a hard-edged disc pattern.

TOOLS, MATERIALS AND REFERENCES

To attempt a more complex model build, the following tools and accessories make the job easier. One of the most important items is a good source of reference material, whether books, drawings, photographs from museums or information from the Internet. The reference source listed at the end of this chapter gives an idea of what is required to embark on a project of this nature.

Styrene sheet, strip, rod, tube and angle of various dimensions were used in the construction of the model. Some of the better hobby shops and model railway stores carry a cornucopia of different sizes of these things, and a good stock of them will come in handy. Also available at model railway shops are Grandt Line nuts, bolts and rivets of various sizes.

In the construction portion of the chapter mention is made of using a lot of parts and pieces from the spares or 'scrap' box. This is an accumulation of material from past projects, and even extra parts included in recent kits that are not intended for that model. Separate kit sprues are available for sale to the consumer, and after using the necessary parts, all the rest becomes part of the inventory of this treasure trove of material. Even old model parts that are inaccurate for their intended use can have bolts and rivets that can be carefully shaved off and put to good use. I had heard from an old wise modeller never to throw anything out, and have benefited from this strategy.

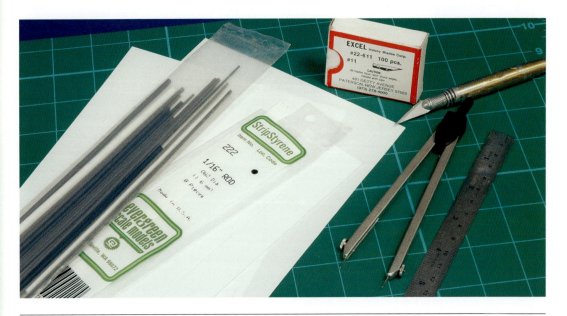

Styrene sheet, rod, tubing and angle in various sizes are necessary to produce some of the parts that tie the project together. Sharp No. 11 hobby blades are important for straight, clean cuts.

Screwdrivers and other tools can be utilized to texture the puttied surface of a model to simulate *Zimmerit,* an anti-magnetic paste applied to some German World War II AFVs.

Assuming one has the basic modelling tools, there are some additional specialized tools that are invaluable when venturing into the world of super-detailing and scratch-building. To properly bend the brass components for fenders, mudflaps and other metal items, an etched-metal bending tool is quite useful. The one that was used for this project was a 4in. version of the Hold and Fold, one of several commercially available tools. When joining etched-metal components together such as the fenders, soldering them makes the strongest bond. A butane soldering tool was purchased at a local electronics shop. The tool has attachments to be used as either a soldering pencil or a blowtorch.

To cut styrene strip at a perfect 90-degree angle a device called the Chopper was used. Once this tool has been set to cut a certain length, numerous sections of styrene can be made with the identical dimensions. This was of great assistance in scratch-building the components for the armoured side skirts.

CONSTRUCTING BRASS FENDERS

Since the kit fenders are moulded with the components of the upper hull that had to be removed, brass fenders from Aber were added to the lower hull tub of the Tamiya Panzer IV. There are two types to choose from, the later ones having the feature of hooking over the wall of the lower hull for solid support. To mount the fenders at the correct height on the hull, a 50- x 50-thou styrene strip was added to the top of the walls.

To assemble the left and right fender sections, the frames were bent into shape using the Hold and Fold. The sections of treadplate were individually soldered into place by cleaning the surfaces with a glass filament brush, and then coating them with flux paste. After positioning the treadplate with small copper clips, slivers of solder were placed near the joints with the flux providing

TOP The lower hull had a styrene shim glued onto the top of the walls to bring the Aber brass fenders to the correct height. Scored sections of styrene sheet replicated the ends of the leaf spring assemblies.

MIDDLE A butane soldering tool was used in the blowtorch mode to fasten the treadplate to the frames of Aber's detail set. Wet tissue paper served as a heat sink on the previously attached panels.

BOTTOM Modelkasten's Late Panzer III/IV Type A track was assembled using 100 links per run.

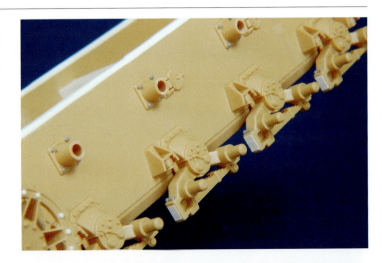

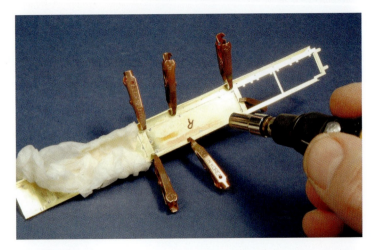

enough 'tack' to keep them in place. Using the soldering tool in the blowtorch mode, the assembly was gently heated up until the solder melted and 'wicked' into the joints. When moving on to the next sections, any adjacent solder joints were protected by either keeping them clipped together, or draping wet tissue paper over them as a heat sink. Care is needed to ensure that the individual treadplate sections start out properly aligned to the frame.

LOWER HULL AND RUNNING GEAR

Tamiya's lower hull tub has a slight bow inward on the walls, and a cross member of 125- x 250-thou styrene was glued in to keep things straight. This was positioned far enough back so as not to interfere with the main gun mount, added later.

The front end of each leaf-spring assembly was detailed by

Casting resin parts

A small number of parts were cast to aid in the construction of this model. Rather than rob unbuilt models of their parts, therefore rendering the kits useless, the required pieces were duplicated in resin using the following method.

To make the mould, an open enclosure was made using children's Lego blocks with a bed of plasticine placed in the bottom. The master part (for example, the cast *Saukopf* mantlet from DML's StuG IIIG kit) was placed in the enclosure and the surface was coated sparingly with a thin layer of mould-release agent. I use Vaseline for this. Silicone rubber was mixed up with a hardening catalyst and poured into the enclosure, first coating the surface of the master to ensure there were no gaps or bubbles. The rubber used was Smooth On Mold Max-30, with similar types being available from General Electric and Dow-Corning. After 24 hours of curing time, the mould can be removed from the enclosure, and the master can be removed from the mould.

Mixing equal parts of Smooth On's Smoothcast 320 in a plastic film canister made two-part epoxy resin. After giving the mould a light coat of Vaseline, the amber liquid was poured into the cavity. A toothpick was used to poke out any bubbles that could be seen while the resin was still runny. After five to ten minutes, the resin hardened into a creamy coloured duplicate mantlet that was removed from the mould.

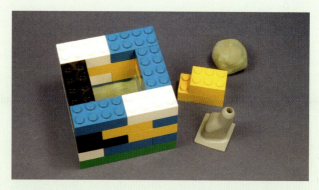

To duplicate DML's *Saukopf* mantlet from their Late StuG IIIG, an enclosure was made from Lego blocks, and the bottom lined with plasticine.

After placing the master in the hole and coating all surfaces with mould-release agent, silicone rubber was mixed with a hardening catalyst and 'painted' onto the part.

After ensuring good coverage with no bubbles, the enclosure was filled with the rubber.

Casting resin parts – continued

After 24 hours, the rubber was cured and the master removed.

Two-part epoxy resin made by 'Smooth On' was mixed in a film canister and poured into the rubber mould.

After approximately ten minutes, the resin is hard enough to remove from the mould, producing a duplicate part to use on the model.

adding a scored section of styrene along with a couple of small bolts. Grease nipples were glued onto the centre of the return rollers. Each return roller mount had the bolt detail replaced with Grandt Line No. 127 bolt heads. The drive sprockets were modified with more accurate bolt detail, adding the missing detail to the inside half, and replacing the outside bolt heads with larger ones made from slicing Plastruct 30-thou styrene hex rod.

Modelkasten's Panzer III/IV Type A tracks (SK-17) replaced the kit's vinyl runs. Each side received 100 links, and the adjustable mounts for the rear idlers were installed to provide the right amount of sag once the runs were installed.

The kit detail for the rear idler adjustment has six-sided nuts. This was corrected by making eight-sided nuts from 30-thou styrene. The kit muffler was replaced with the later flame suppressor stacks made from 4mm aluminium tubing. Smaller styrene tubing with fins was inserted into these, and the assembly was supported at the correct angle with styrene strip. The kit's base for each exhaust stack was supported by a styrene strip, which was bent to shape with tweezers and detailed with Grandt Line's No. 127 bolts. Small brass chain was used as retainers for the two towing pins at the front of the vehicle, and caps on the rear plate.

UPPER HULL AND FIGHTING COMPARTMENT

The rear engine deck and front glacis plate were salvaged from the upper hull of the Panzer IVJ kit. These parts were carefully removed with a razor saw, leaving excess plastic that would later be filed down flat to the correct fit. The fighting compartment from Tamiya's StuG IIIG kit was removed from its upper hull kit part in the same fashion. Using reference drawings and photographs, the components were test fitted on the lower hull and fender assembly. By supporting the rear of the fighting compartment on a styrene strip, it was positioned for correct height and cemented to the engine deck. The area between the front glacis plate and the fighting compartment had a flat steel plate that overlapped the fenders on each side, and this was made with 15-thou styrene sheet. Where the rear plate of the engine deck meets the lower hull a thin strip of 10-thou styrene strip was cemented in place as the upper part of the joining flange. Bolt detail was added to this on the upper and lower faces. The upper rear plate was modified to have brackets for the tow cable, and also brass hangers were added on the top for spare track stowage.

The engine deck's hatch handles were replaced with ones fashioned from solder wire. The ends were squashed flat and bolt detail added to them. The perimeter of the hatches had flush rivet detail added to match photo references taken of a Jagdpanzer IV at the Aberdeen Proving Grounds in Maryland, USA. The small styrene discs were made using a 23-thou punch on 5-thou sheet. The engine air intakes at the side received small bent brass strips added to the top as clips for the sectional covers.

The fighting compartment sat higher on the Panzer IV chassis than it did on the Panzer III. To close the resulting gap, metal plating skirted the lower portion to join the fenders. Styrene sheet was used to model this feature, along with hexagonal headed bolts that were shaved from the bottom of the Panzer IVJ hull. The plating showed a gap near the fenders where it met the walls of the fighting compartment. Additional trim was placed around the perimeter of the skirt, and hex nuts glued onto this.

StuG IVs were modified at the driver's position with an armoured cab equipped with two periscopes and a hatch on the roof. The original front armour plating from the StuG III was left in place, and a cutout was made behind the driver's head. The cab was built from cutting a 60-thou styrene front plate and positioning it at the back edge of the glacis. Sections of 20-thou styrene were cut for the remaining sides and top according to drawings, and trimmed to fit ensuring that the joints were recessed for the addition of weld beads (almost unnecessary since *Zimmerit* application would cover this later). A later style crew hatch was engraved onto the roof using a needle, with help from a metal drafting template to get the corners rounded. Periscope tops were taken from the spares box — unused extras from a previous Tamiya Panther G project. The periscope covers were made from thick lead sheet taken from a ski-wax container. The hinges for the hatch were resin copies from the hatch detail of the DML StuG IIIB kit. Smaller resin parts like this are best located into position with liquid styrene cement, and then secured with a touch of cyano glue.

Later StuG IV vehicles were equipped with the remotely fired MG34 *Rundumfeuer* and the vehicle being modelled had this feature. The mount for the MG34 was made from Aber's etched-metal parts from a detail set for the Hetzer, and styrene base and shields. The tensioning spring for the trigger was made from thin copper wire wound around a small drill bit. The 10-thou styrene used for the shield was flexible enough to be bent at the front without breaking using a pair of tweezers and some patient coaxing. The loader's hatch was re-configured to accommodate the *Rundumfeuer* by opening to the sides rather than forward and back. New hatches were cut from styrene sheet and given rivet and lock detail. The flush rivets were made by pressing a syringe needle that had been cut flat and reamed to a thin edge down into the plastic. Resin cast hinges were also added to the hatches. Also mounted on the roofs of later StuGs was the *Nahverteidigungswaffe* (close-quarters defence weapon). This part of the model was taken from the Panzer IVJ kit, since they had them mounted on the turret roof. Five *Pilze* hoist mounts were added to the roof using small sections of 75-thou styrene tube cut at an angle to match the slope.

The commander's hatch was detailed with a copper wire pull

The glacis plate from the Panzer IVJ kit was removed from the upper hull and mounted in the lower hull. A styrene support rod ensured the hull was not bowed in the centre.

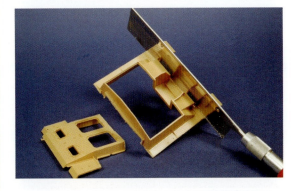

A razor saw helped remove the superstructure from Tamiya's StuG IIIG kit.

The StuG IIIG fighting compartment, along with the upper engine compartment from the Panzer IVJ, were carefully aligned and glued into place.

handle and two locking levers made from styrene. The small supports in between each periscope were given four small rivets. Each of these tiny rivets was shaved from a Tamiya Marder III gun cradle from the spares box.

The mount from Tamiya's StuG IIIG kit was adapted to the resin mantlet, and glued onto the floor of the lower hull. The mount had to be trimmed down by 2mm to allow the gun to sit at the correct height. Hooks for a weather cover made from brass runner from an etched-metal detail set were cemented to the rear of the mantlet, and also the front of the upper hull behind the gun. The main gun was a turned aluminium barrel with a brass muzzle brake

The kit's exhaust was replaced with the stacks seen on later Panzer IVs. The support fins for the inner pipes were made from 5-thou styrene.

Small springs were made by winding extremely thin copper wire around a No. 76 drill bit. The wire was taken from the cord from an old lamp.

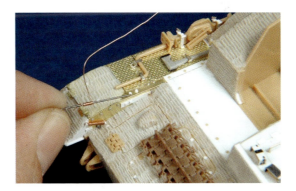

The remote MG mount was pieced together with spare brass detail from an old Aber Hetzer set and styrene base and shields. The later configuration of the loader's hatches had them opening to the sides to accommodate the MG34.

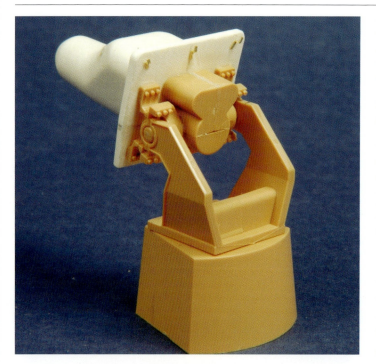

TOP The gun mount from Tamiya's StuG IIIG kit was modified to fit the resin *Saukopf* mantlet. Brass clips for the weather cover were fashioned from brass strip.

BOTTOM To complete the forward portion of the fighting compartment, a driver's position was scratch built using various thicknesses of styrene. If the necessary thickness was not available, pieces were laminated to provide the appropriate size. Reference drawings determined the slope and dimension of the sections, and parts were trimmed to fit using trial and error.

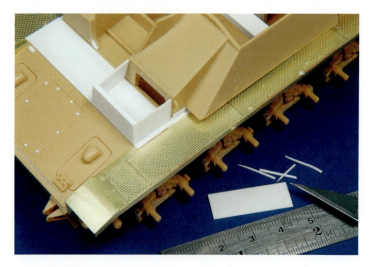

cut to 57mm was cemented onto each base as a final step of construction once the model had been painted and weathered. These fragile items would have broken off numerous times otherwise.

The spare roadwheel bin was constructed from styrene sheet, and mounted on brackets that raised it from the fender. A spare track bar was mounted at the very top of the right-hand side of the fighting compartment. Some drawings have shown the bracket to be similar to the Panzer IV though mounted lower, but other than the prototype StuG IV the production vehicles appear to have just the one bar with any spares hanging from the link above it.

ZIMMERIT

There are a number of ways to simulate the *Zimmerit* anti-magnetic paste, which was applied to German vehicles for a time during World War II. Thin sections of

from a German company called Army in Detail.

Antennae mounts were used from the Tamiya StuG III kit, and additional bolt detail was placed on the left-hand mount. The one on the right-hand side actually had the bolts inside of the enclosure. The base of the antennae was from DML's German Tank Antenna Set kit (3819), which features the wing-nut fasteners. Stretched sprue

pre-made *Zimmerit* in resin and brass, and replacement parts featuring the texture, are commercially available. Some models, especially in 1/72 scale, have it already moulded onto the kit. The best way I know of to apply *Zimmerit* to a model is by using Zimm-It-Rite two-part epoxy putty by R&J Enterprises, USA. Although the task of applying this texture to a model seems rather daunting, the job goes easily if it's done a section at a time.

Enough of the putty was removed from the two containers and combined to make a lump the size of a pea. This was placed onto the surface of the model and worked flat with a toothpick or screwdriver, attempting to get as thin a layer as possible. The texture was applied by pressing the end of a screwdriver into the putty, and repeating in straight lines, as per the pattern on a real vehicle. Care was taken to keep the material clear of hinges, bolt heads and fittings. The next adjacent area was done in the same fashion, re-texturing the overlap to give a seamless appearance.

SCRATCH-BUILDING ARMOURED SIDE SKIRTS

The Germans started to use side skirts, or *Schürzen*, as a result of the Russian anti-tank rifles on the Eastern Front. Some aftermarket companies produce etched-brass skirts in the solid or mesh form, but they are simple to reproduce in styrene.

Drawings from the Spielberger book *Sturmgeschütz and its Variants* were

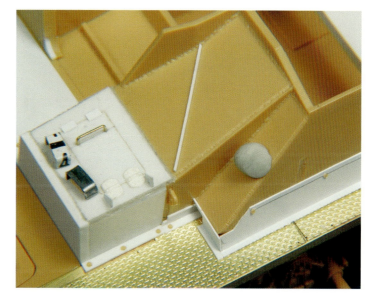

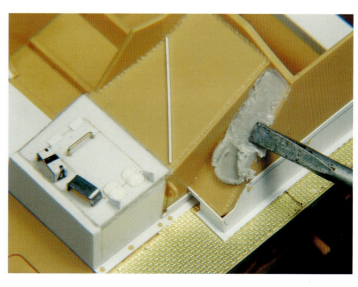

TOP After completing the structural detail, *Zimmerit* texture was applied to the model with R&J Enterprises Zimm-It Rite epoxy putty.

BOTTOM The *Zimmerit* process was accomplished a small section at a time. Putty was kneaded into a ball the size of a pea, and spread onto the surface of the model making it as thin and even as possible.

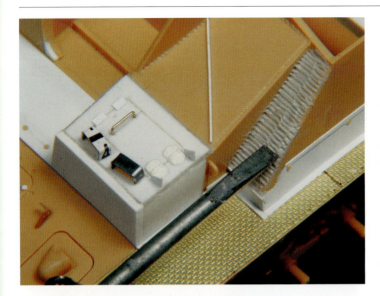

TOP Following photos of the actual vehicle, the surface was textured using a screwdriver, creating ridges that ran parallel to the ground. The rows of ridges were kept as straight as possible, and overlaps were re-worked to show continuous texture.

BOTTOM When dry, the putty can be lifted off to appear chipped and battle damaged.

The top hangers of the Schürzen were made from bending aluminium strip on a former made from a piece of styrene. The lower bracket was made from styrene strip. To ensure all of the brackets were of identical dimensions, the strip was cut using the Chopper tool that also affirms a 90-degree angle on each cut. The hangers on the fenders were built to represent the production style, as opposed to the ones shown in drawings of the prototype.

The rivets for all of the skirt brackets were sliced from the lower hulls of older kits. Many obsolete kits can be picked up for bargain prices at model club swap meets and other venues, and are an economical source of such parts.

The Schürzen were mounted on the model to test fit the locations of the hangers and supports, and were labelled with a pencil since there were slight differences to each of the sections. The panels were mounted on the vehicle such that they were pulled in towards the bottom by the hangers mounted on the edge of the fenders. They had

studied to get the correct dimensions of the skirt and bracket hardware. Sections of 10-thou styrene were cut for the individual Schürzen, taking into account the angle at which they're drawn, and the fact that they were each overlapped by a millimetre (in 1/35 scale). The rails that hung the Schürzen were cut from Evergreen 60-thou styrene angle. The brackets that mounted the rail to the vehicle were made from 10- x 60-thou styrene strip, and built to match the dimensions of the StuG IIIG brackets in the Tamiya kit.

The Chopper was used to cut styrene strip to make the brackets for the side skirts, or *Schürzen*. Consistent cuts at a 90-degree angle ensure that the parts are identical in dimension.

The *Schürzen* were made from 10-thou styrene sheet, and overlapped each other at the rear by approximately 1mm. The upper brackets were bent from aluminium strip, and the lower ones from styrene strip.

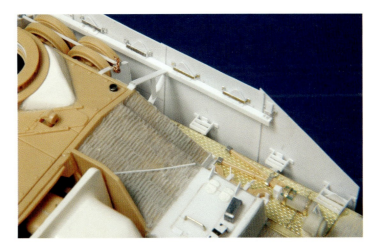

The rails on which the side skirts were mounted were made from Evergreen styrene angle. The shovel was given a brass strip mounting bracket, and was positioned with the blade to the rear, which differed from the configuration on the Panzer IV.

the option of swinging out perpendicular to the ground when the wider *Ostketten* or *Winterketten* tracks were used.

DETAILING THE FENDERS AND MUDFLAPS

The Aber fender detail sets come with the rear mudflaps but not the front ones. These were made from styrene sheet and given a half-round lip on the edge using shaved-down 20-thou styrene rod. Both the front and rear mudflaps were held in place with a spring, and the springs were fashioned from very thin copper wire wound around a No. 76 drill bit. The rear mudflaps had a rounded lip that followed the lower edge of the inside cover, and this was made by shaving a length of solder wire down to half-round, then gluing it along the bent contour.

Following the layout in the reference drawings in the Spielberger book, the vehicle's tools were attached to the model. Other than Aber's photo-etched tool clamps, the mounting brackets for the tools were built from styrene strip and Modelkasten wing nuts. The 10-thou Evergreen strip has a more authentic thickness compared to some of the thin etched-brass offerings from the aftermarket companies. Aber's workable tool clamps did require some patience to assemble, but once the technique had been practised a few times the process went quickly. Tamiya's tools from the Panzer IVJ sufficed for most of the on-vehicle equipment, and a small pry bar was made from a length of solder wire. The resin body and etched-brass fasteners from Royal Model's German Fire Extinguisher detail set were combined with some plastic parts for the fire extinguisher mounted behind the Royal Model's resin headlamp. The axe was a DML tool, and it was mounted with its handle partway under the right-hand side of the superstructure.

PAINTING, MARKINGS AND WEATHERING

To handle the model during the painting and weathering process, I screwed a file handle into the lower hull. I modified the file handle by gluing a wood screw into the orifice. This provided a steady base to work the paint from all angles without having to touch the surface.

I began by airbrushing on a primer coat of Floquil paints mixed into a very dark brown. Serving as a pre-shading step, this lacquer-based paint provides a solid base on all the multimedia parts. It allows a homogenous surface on which to lay down the subsequent acrylic colours of the final coats. The vehicle and all other

The armoured deflector at the front of the cupola was resin cast from a DML StuG III part. On the actual vehicle, the fittings on the side of the hull were welded to the very edge of the upper walls so that the roof could be removed for maintenance.

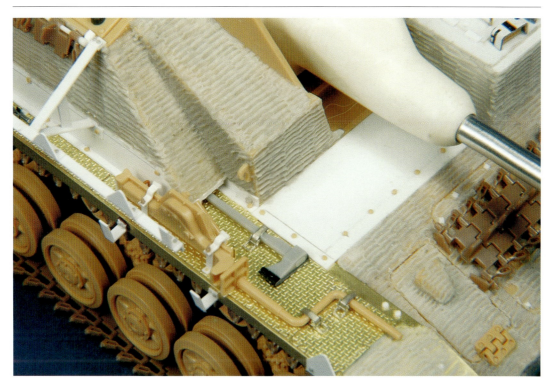

BELOW The Modelkasten track links were installed on the kit and the rear idlers adjusted to obtain a realistic 'sag' over the return rollers.

ABOVE Some of the tool stowage brackets were scratch-built from styrene strip, which will bend and hold its shape if done carefully. The clamps for the axe and starter crank were the newer Aber workable brass ones.

The model was held during the painting process by drilling a hole in the lower hull, and inserting a wooden file handle, which had been modified to hold a wood screw. A fine dusting of diluted dirt colour was sprayed over the whole model to tone down the freshly painted look.

accessories including the wheels and side skirts were primed this way.

For the main coat of paint for the model, I applied a water-based paint. This is to ensure that the oil-based spirit used for the weathering process does not adversely affect the finish. The base coat for the three-colour camouflage was airbrushed onto the parts after the primer had cured for 48 hours. A mixture of Tamiya's acrylic XF-60 Dark Yellow and XF-59 Desert Yellow was combined in a 4:1 ratio. This made a colour I was satisfied with as a match for *dunkelgelb* after referencing an original piece of equipment. The paint was diluted with Tamiya's acrylic thinner by 1:1, and sprayed on lightly with an air pressure of 30psi set on the compressor's regulator. The paint has to be lightly applied to allow some of the undercoat primer to show through, providing some depth and shadow to the details and contours of the model.

For the camouflage on the vehicle, bands of green and brown were airbrushed in a random pattern leaving a soft demarcation at the edges. Model Master acrylic Panzer Olivgrün and Tamiya's Red Brown mixed with some black were applied in succession, each being thinned down 3:1 with the majority of the mix being thinner. With the paint being this diluted, a fairly tight edge can be achieved, but it does take some patience to cover the entire model with the desired pattern. The wheels and other separate accessories were also painted in the same fashion. Tools and other details were all painted at this point. Spare tracks and the metal parts of the shovel, axe and pry bars were picked out in a steel colour. Periscopes were painted black, and the tyres on the roadwheels were painted in a very dark grey.

To paint the spots on the *Schürzen*, a mask was made from a section of 10-thou styrene sheet. Two different-size holes were punched into the plastic in a random configuration using a Waldron punch and die set. The resulting template was taped onto the skirts and frequently re-positioned for airbrushing on the green and brown pattern. Tamiya's masking tape is the best material I've found for this purpose, since it stays where it's put, and doesn't lift the finish when removed.

The areas where the national insignia were to be applied was painted with Tamiya's acrylic gloss. Waterslide decals were the weapon of choice due to the rough *Zimmerit* surface. Using Tamiya's aftermarket decal sheet 'E', the markings were soaked and removed from the backing, and carefully placed into position using Solvaset decal setting solution. This aggressive liquid softens the decal film so that it relaxes over every contour, but once it is applied there is very little

For the disc camouflage on the *Schürzen*, a mask was made by randomly punching holes into styrene sheet.

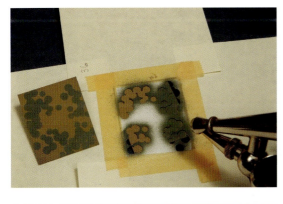

The process of painting the discs on the *Schürzen* involved moving the mask numerous times each time when spraying on each colour.

To add a muddy look to the lower part of the model, MIG Productions' acrylic modelling paste was mixed with pastel powders and static grass, and randomly applied to the surface with an old brush.

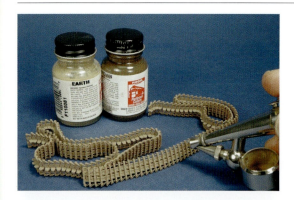

Painting the tracks first involved coating them with a layer of Floquil paint. The dirt colour was made from a mixture of Earth and Roof Brown.

After grounding up various colours of chalk pastels, they were mixed with Tamiya's acrylic thinner and daubed randomly onto both sides of the track runs.

Each track run was dry-brushed aggressively with a combination of Humbrol enamel silver and steel colours, showing bare metal surface at the point of contact with ground and running gear. Care was taken to not allow the silver to look too garish.

time to manoeuvre the marking into place. Once the decals had dried, a clear flat coat was airbrushed onto the surface using Model Master Flat Lacquer.

The first step in weathering the model was the application of an overall coat of a dirty coloured acrylic paint, diluted with about 95 per cent thinner. Tamiya Buff, Earth, Deck Tan and Khaki Drab were mixed and sprayed over the entire model with extra emphasis on the running gear, rear plate, fenders, and any other areas that would typically collect dust. The intention of this is to 'tone down' the look of the model and blend the components.

Working a small section at a time, a large paintbrush was used

ABOVE The model received a random daubing of earth-coloured pastel chalks to simulate the accumulation of dust and dirt in its nether regions.

LEFT Small areas of chipped paint were simulated by mixing a dark brown Vallejo watercolour, and applying it to appropriate locations with a fine-tipped 000 brush.

The model's smaller details were enhanced by a wash of raw umber oil paint. This was diluted with ordinary paint thinner and applied to the dampened surface of the model in small sections.

Modle Master's Panzer Olivgrün speckles were painted into the areas between the disc-pattern camouflage on the *Schürzen* using an old brush.

The particular StuG IV modelled had *Zimmerit* also applied to the lower hull between the wheel mounts.

The tyres of the kit were painted using Floquil's Weathered Black, which is actually a very dark grey.

ABOVE Humbrol's silver enamel was toned down with a small amount of raw umber oil paint, and lightly dry-brushed over certain spots to give them a worn metal look. Spare tracks, tools and the gun mantlet were given some of this treatment.

LEFT After the markings were applied, they were sprayed with Testors' Model Master Flat Lacquer to give them a matt finish.

Small brass chain from Tiger Model Designs was used for the retaining devices on the vehicle. Dark pastel powder helped give the surface of the exhaust stacks a burnt look.

The figures added to the project came from the Tristar and DML lines. Resin heads were added to the ground troops since they offer very life-like facial features and correctly shaped helmets. Small strips of lead sheet were used for the gun slings.

should be approached cautiously by pausing and examining the work as it progresses.

DISPLAYING THE MODEL IN A VIGNETTE WITH FIGURES

Displaying a model on a base with realistic groundwork adds to the realism of the finished piece. To add figures gives the vehicle some perspective, and brings life to the scene. The model was placed in a setting to show its role of infantry support by adding a commander and a couple of walking Panzergrenadiers depicting how things would look in Germany during the cold spring of 1945.

Tristar's Self-Propelled Gun Crew Set Vol. 2 provided the commander for the StuG IV, complete with field grey panzer wrap and wedge cap. He was painted by first priming the face with Testors' Flat Desert Tan enamel, and then completing the features in oil paints after that had dried for a few days. His field grey uniform was painted with Vallejo watercolours, mixing 888 Olive Grey with varying amounts of black and white to complete the shading and highlighting. The piping on the

to dampen the surface of the model with paint thinner. Using a smaller brush loaded with thinned raw umber oil paint, a 'wash' was applied to various areas of detail like hinges, rivets and bolts, engine and crew hatches. To prevent 'tide marks', an additional larger dry brush was used to wipe the areas. This was also effective in creating rain marks, if the brush was dragged in a downward fashion pulling the excess paint with it. The entire surface of the model was worked in this way, so that the effect appeared even. Both sides of the *Schürzen* were washed in this manner, with the wash being applied somewhat thicker to give a more streaked appearance.

Small paint scratches were simulated by mixing Vallejo's Black and Hull Red watercolours, and applying them with a fine-tipped 000 paint brush. In addition to demonstrating wear and tear, this technique enhances detail and defines some of the smaller parts. It can also be easily over done, and similar to any weathering method,

For creating the groundwork for the vignette, a papier-mâché product called Celluclay, paint pigment, and white glue were mixed together with a small amount of water.

A walnut trophy base was masked and sanded down with a course grade of paper to allow the groundwork to adhere.

After spreading a thin layer of the Celluclay mixture onto the base, various colours of static grass and small grit were sprinkled onto the surface and patted down. The vinyl track runs from the Panzer IVJ model were then pressed into the wet mixture to form a spot for the model to sit. Toothpicks marked the locations where the figures would be mounted.

colour tabs and shoulder boards was picked out in a dull red to indicate the service detachment of the self-propelled gun crews.

Two DML figures wearing the insulated parka and pants combination were modified with resin heads from Warriors and Hornet. The aftermarket heads provided an additional level of detail and expression to the faces, and had a more correct helmet shape than the injection-moulded plastic ones. After finishing the faces using oil paints, the uniforms were painted in the standard army splinter camouflage using various mixtures of Vallejo watercolours. Different shades of the base colour were mixed to show a variety to the splinter pattern, and the figures were sprayed with a thinned mixture of dirt-coloured acrylic to slightly tone down the vivid pattern when complete.

A wooden trophy base had the edges masked and the surface sanded down to prepare it for the groundwork. A mixture of Celluclay, white PVA glue, and paint pigment were stirred up with a little water, and spread onto the roughed-up surface. Keeping the

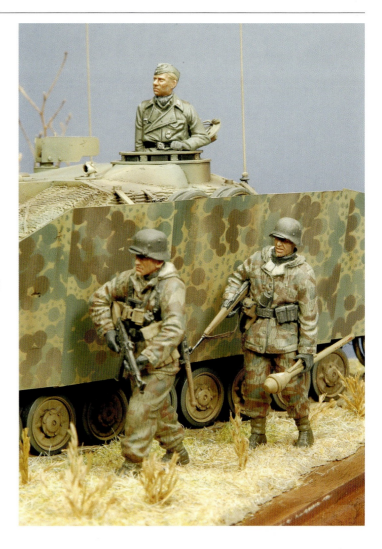

RIGHT The infantry figures are shown wearing their padded parka and pants combination, finished in the standard army splinter scheme of brown with green patches, and darker green rain marks.

OPPOSITE TOP After positioning all of the components of the vignette, additional vegetation was added in the form of small dried plants. The small tufts were wetted with white glue, and placed randomly around the base.

OPPOSITE BOTTOM The vehicle is shown in one of its primary roles of infantry support late in World War II.

groundwork layer thin, fine grit and static grass of various colours were spread onto the surface and pushed down with a stiff brush. The vinyl track runs from the Panzer IVJ kit were pressed into the wet groundwork after the final position of the model was determined, then removed before locating the model into place. After drilling the appropriate locating holes into the base, the two Panzergrenadier figures had a hole drilled up into their feet and a section of thick wire glued in to secure them. Small tufts of dried plants were dipped into the PVA glue and placed randomly onto the base. Larger limbs were grouped in behind the vehicle to indicate uncleared bush, still bare from the recent winter.

The completed vignette took three months of spare time to complete, and I'd like to thank my good friend Tom Cockle for his invaluable assistance with this project.

References

Bitoh, Mitsuru, *Achtung Panzer 5* (Dai Nippon Kaiga Publishing: Tokyo, 1992)
Ledwoch, Janusz, *Sturmgeschütz IV* (Wydawnictwo Militaria: Warsaw, 1999)
Jentz, Tom, and Doyle, Hilary, *New Vanguard 37: Sturmgeschütz III and IV 1942–45*, (Osprey Publishing Ltd: Oxford, 2001)
Spielberger, Walter J., *Sturmgeschütz and its Variants* (Schiffer Publishing Ltd: Atglen, PA, 1993)

IDF TIRAN 5 MAIN BATTLE TANK

BY NICK CORTESE

This chapter illustrates the construction and painting of a 1/35-scale model of the Israeli Tiran 5 MBT, based on a captured Egyptian or Syrian T-55. This build uses as its base the excellent Tamiya T-55A and shows how to combine resin upgrade sets with a basic kit to create a whole new variant. It also includes a large number of scratch-built and photo-etched parts to complete the model, and details a number of painting and finishing techniques.

INTRODUCTION

Blast Models' Tiran 5 set consists of over 100 resin pieces cast in a cream resin colour. This set offers three options: Tiran 4, Tiran 5 and the SLA Tiran 5, and the version modelled here is the Tiran 5, or TI-67. The overall quality of Blast Models' upgrade set is excellent; however, some parts appear to be a little vague and simplified in terms of detail, while the larger resin parts are somewhat marred in some areas. However, these deficiencies can be remedied with a bit of styrene, Mr Surfacer and a lot of patience.

Tamiya's kit of the T-55 has to be one of the best ever produced, with state-of-the-art build quality and fit; even so, there is always room for a few improvements.

TOOLS

When working with resin good X-Acto knives and files of all sizes are a must for cleaning up any flash and smoothing out bits. Sanding sticks are also a must, and I use the Squadron brand that come in a multipack of all the different grit grades.

Joining pieces of resin together needs a good solid glue, and for this project I used Zap-A-Gap thin and medium cyanoacrylate glues, which are available in most hobby shops. Attaching small parts is easy: just dab a couple of drops of the glue onto a clean small glass area and wait for about a minute; then, using a sharpened toothpick, add a small amount to the model part. Afterwards, depending on the part, I usually brush on some

HISTORY

After the victories of the Six-Day War (1967) and the Yom Kippur War (1973), the Israeli Defence Forces (IDF) captured hundreds of mostly Egyptian and Syrian T-54 and T-55 main battle tanks, and decided to convert them for use by their own forces.

The captured tanks were renamed Tiran after an island in the Red Sea – Tiran 4 based on the T-54 and Tiran 5 based on the T-55; an alternative designation was TI-67 (Tank Israeli-1967).

The modifications made to the tanks included the upgrading of the main armament from 100 to 105mm and the addition of 30 and 50mm machine guns to the turret, not to mention a plethora of storage bins. Throughout their service history in the IDF the Tirans were painted in a progression of different sand-based colours, starting with a light sand and progressing through to a grey-green colour. In the late 1970s, many Tirans were sold to the South Lebanese Army, who usually kept the 100mm main armament. These vehicles were usually painted a light blue colour.

liquid cement as well as a bit of Mr Surfacer 500 to seal the part. Most important when working with cyanoacrylate glues and resin is to work in a well-ventilated room, wear a respirator, or simply do what I do to keep resin dust down to a minimum: sand all your resin bits with or in water; simply dousing your sanding stick in water before sanding will help to keep the dust to a minimum.

TURRET

Before starting construction, I gently soaked both main kit sprues in warm soapy water and let them dry overnight. This helped clean both the plastic and resin surfaces of any mould-release oils.

To start things off, I removed all the 100-plus resin parts from their respective casting blocks and organized them into sections. This gets most of the resin dust issue out of the way at the beginning. I stored the parts in small, sealable plastic jars with appropriate labels. This makes it easy to find the right bits later on in the building process.

I began construction on this project by cleaning up and smoothing out the details on the surface of the turret. The next task was to properly site the two resin turret antennae mounts, ensuring through test fitting that they lined up correctly with the rear turret bustle. As per the Blast Models instructions, I drew a line down the back of the turret which lined up the IDF bustle with the rear of the turret; if done properly this should ensure that both antennae are positioned correctly.

ITEMS USED

Tamiya T-55A (35257)
Blast Models IDF Tiran 5 resin upgrade set (BL35019K)
Verlinden Productions T-55 Resin engine and compartment set (2186)
WWII Productions resin T-55 workable tracks (35008)
Verlinden Productions dry transfer set IDF vehicle markings No. 1
Verlinden Productions Israeli ID etch plates
MIG Productions various dry transfer numbers
Eduard photo-etch (TP043)
Evergreen sheet stock (various sizes)
Plastruct rod and strip (various sizes)
Tichy Train plastic bolt heads and rivets
Karaya Modern Russian Tow Cables (KTC 35006)

The first step in construction is filling in and sanding smooth the surface detail of the turret, as well as removing the moulded line feed for the IR searchlight, which will be replaced with styrene rod. I replaced the kit-supplied turret grab handles with 0.15in. brass wire, which is more in scale than the kit-supplied items.

To keep a uniform overall foundation to work upon, I applied a completely new casting effect to the turret with Mr Surfacer 1000, which is stippled on with a nylon brush.

The turret is starting to take shape. The rear antennae mounts have been attached. Take note that they need to be perfectly aligned with the back bustle to fit perfectly.

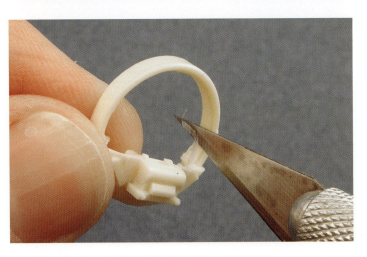

Carefully remove excess resin flash from the interior area of the commander's cupola hatch using a sharp X-Acto knife.

A slight gap between the resin and kit part of the commander's cupola was evident. Much like Mr Surfacer, Tamiya Liquid Surface Primer is thin enough that capillary action fills up the gap perfectly.

The Tiran commander's cupola assembled, detailed and ready for painting. I've added Tichy Train bolt heads and rivets to the .30-cal. MG and mount bow arm area.

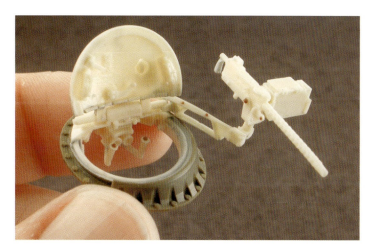

The loader's hatch hinge area is getting the proper welds, using pieces of stretched sprue. These are softened with a coat of liquid glue, and then carefully cut with a sharp X-Acto knife; a final quick coat of liquid glue seals the weld bead.

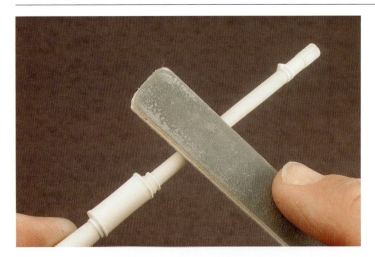

Sanding the two-piece 105mm resin gun smooth. The resin had some inconsistencies in areas. Using a fine sanding stick, I carefully sanded back and forth to get a nice smooth barrel. Add a couple of drops of water when sanding: not only is it better health wise, but helps with resin build-up on the sanding stick itself.

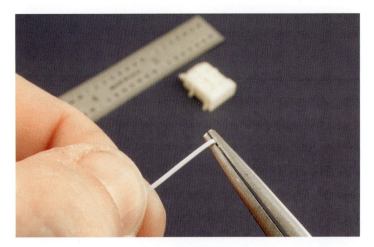

Fabricating a turret empty jerrycan holder. 10 x 20-thou strip was used to replicate the metal jerrycan holder bracing. The building begins with a nice straight bend using needle-nose pliers, then going back to the original resin part for exact size and carefully bending the other side to match.

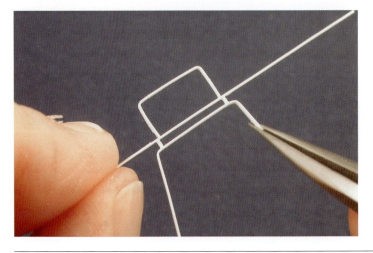

The top portion of the jerrycan bracing set after gluing. The attachment rods to the inner portion are 20-thou styrene rod.

After the glue was fully dry, I carefully removed the inner portion with the help of straight nail clippers.

The top bracing can now be attached to the lower bin area, which was made in the same manner using measured styrene sheet. Tichy Train bolts and bent 34-gauge soft wire were used to replicate the tie-downs.

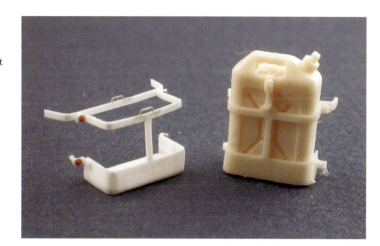

Next to the four-tube flag mount, I positioned an empty fire extinguisher mount made from styrene and brass bits from the spares box.

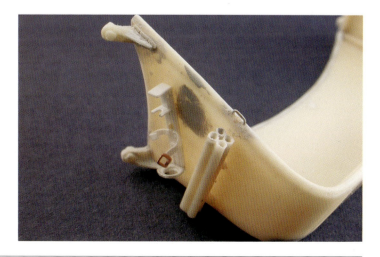

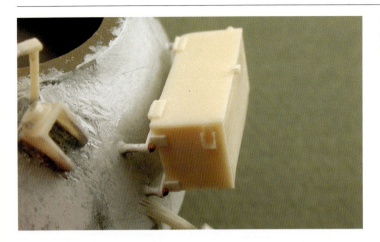

Blast Models' turret bin did not have any proper attachment mounts. I made four new mounts from 25-thou rod.

IR searchlight detail: I removed the searchlight cover and detailed the mount with proper bracing, and replaced the moulded-on IR feed line from the turret top with styrene rod.

This view shows the completed turret prior to painting. I scratch-built the turret top tie-downs once more with soft 34-gauge wire. Blast Models offer these tie-downs in resin, but they are over scale and unconvincing.

The Blast Models set gives you a nice set of IDF-modified loader's and driver's hatches, which require further detailing in the form of brass handles and the like.

The commander's hatch resin details are quite impressive, notably the extended 30mm machine-gun mount and internal hatch detail.

I wanted to display the internal main sights of the commander's hatch, so I left the hatch open.

The loader's hatch inner ring simply fits into place as the middle of the piece has a wafer-thin resin coating that protects it. This inner portion is then carefully removed with a sharp X-Acto blade.

I replaced the rather over-proportioned Blast Models resin tie-downs with soft wire, which I simply bent to shape with the tip of my needle-nose pliers then cut to size and shape. As per the instructions, I measured the distance between each tie-down and carefully attached them with a tiny amount of CA glue. As you can see by the photos of the turret, I applied a mix of Tamiya extra-thin cement and Mr Surfacer 500 to each individual tie-down for added strength and uniformity.

Blast Models' IDF 105mm L7 gun is supplied in two resin pieces. All that is required after assembly is a bit of cleanup. Blast Models also supplies the gun mantlet, which replicates the IDF-applied canvas material perfectly and fits to the turret without a problem.

The remainder of the turret attachments are pretty straightforward, though it's always worth double-checking the placement before gluing the pieces on.

A quick tip for gluing small parts, be they resin or photo-etch, is to use a mixture of Tamiya extra-thin cement and Mr Surfacer 500 as mentioned above. This mixture enables you to attach a piece and move it into position before confirming the location with CA glue.

When the main items were glued into place I proceeded to add the appropriate welds to all the items for a realistic subtle look. To give the model additional character I incorporated some simple scratch-built details, such as a couple of empty jerrycan holders and an empty fire extinguisher holder.

HULL

Tamiya's lower hull suspension was quickly cleaned up and assembled in about an hour's time before being set aside to dry. As per the Blast Models instructions, I filled in the back glacis bracket portion with styrene rod and sealed it with Tamiya surfacer before sanding it smooth

At this point, I proceeded to add the proper welds to the fender bracings and top hull area. Many modellers omit this subtle detail

but I feel it gives a more realistic look to the kit even though most of the welds cannot be seen outright. The weld beads were easily created by using small pieces of stretched sprue softened with Tamiya extra-thin cement.

Some careful surgery is required to remove the original kit front fenders to make way for the resin IDF replacements. At the same time I also decided to remove the kit moulded rear mudflaps, instead opting to scratch-build new items.

Moving to the T-55 external fuel cell area, I fabricated all the much-needed plumbing out of styrene rod as well as the fuel cell attachments out of various sizes of styrene strip.

I was lucky to have an extra engine deck from a previous project, so I used it to my advantage. Along with the Verlinden-supplied resin hatches I opened the hatch areas up, adding the internal lip, and subsequently used this part to display the open engine detail.

VERLINDEN T-55 RESIN ENGINE

As with the Blast kit's resin parts, I cleaned up and stored each part in sections beforehand. Construction was straightforward; I started with the engine block mounts first and added styrene detail as I went. Working in subassemblies I made sure that the main components fitted together nicely before

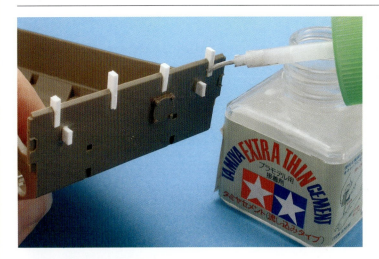

All IDF Tirans had the two large rear fuel tanks and supports removed. As per the instructions, I filled in the area using styrene strips and sealed with liquid cement.

The IDF replaced the all-metal T-55 front fenders with a semi-rubber type that Blast Models recreates beautifully. Some simple surgery is required to remove the kit fender, and the fit is perfect. I made the front fender torsion bars from 12-thou brass rod with Athabasca brass eyelet connecting points carefully drilled in and glued into place.

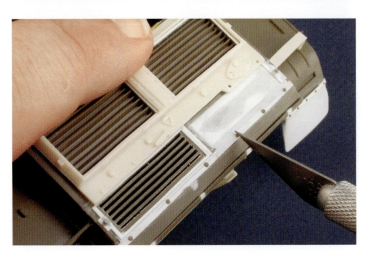

Detailing the rear engine deck: Most Tirans are either Polish- or Czech-built T-55s. The rear deck needs to be tweaked a bit for added detail and fit. I filled in the rear portion vent portions and added a new 'rear edge', which was detailed with styrene strip and bolts from the spares box to get it looking better.

Adding the fuel lines: many modellers use brass or copper wire to replicate the fender fuel tank lines. I use 15-thou styrene rod for the main fuel lines and tiny pieces of 20-thou rod for the line clamp fittings.

Removing the attachment points from the loader's tool bin: with a sharp X-Acto knife I carefully remove the rather bland resin attachment points.

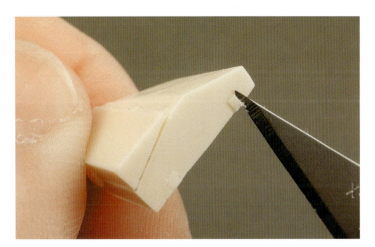

New attachment points are made from styrene strip and rod as well as Tichy Train nut and bolt detail. For consistency, I replaced every stowage bin in this manner

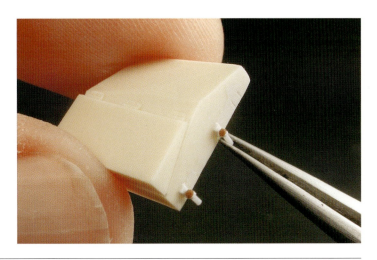

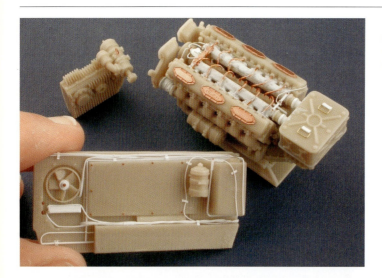

Verlinden makes an easy-to-build and pretty accurate T-55 engine. Here it is detailed with various styrene and brass items.

Sanding the resin engine hatches: cutting down the resin is made easy using wet-dry sandpaper doused in water. A circular motion with even pressure will give a nice even area.

Verlinden's V2 engine starts to get some paint. After a pre-shading of Tamiya XF69 Nato Black a coating of Tamiya XF20 Medium Grey was sprayed on. I carefully applied Vallejo 814 Burnt Cadmium Red to the engine valve covers as well as the air filter area.

I used Citadel Mithril Silver sponged on for the worn chipping effect. A couple of oil wash applications as well as some pastel dust brings the engine to life. You can almost hear the 560hp diesel engine roar.

A view of the engine installed with the hatches in the open position.

Another view with the engine deck removed. The kit-supplied thermal shield exhaust cover is actually a bit too thick. I simply burnished a piece of foil over the kit-supplied item, cut to shape then attached for a more realistic in scale look.

Rear upper area details. I used Eduard's T-55 Zoom etch set mainly for the rear screens which are acceptable. I removed the moulded-on rear mudflaps and replaced them with detailed scratch-built styrene items.

Hull front area details. I added the proper conduits for the front headlight wiring from 20-thou rod. I also had to fabricate a new protective light guard cover, as well as the attachments, mainly because the original resin supplied item it very delicate and had crumbled apart. Verlinden's etch IDF ID plates are a nice touch; unfortunately the serial number doesn't match this exact vehicle, but we can't have everything!

Rear upper area details. Here is a clear view of the completed styrene fuel lines as well as both scratch-built tow cable locks. The Karaya T-55 tow cable's resin lifting eye is carefully attached to the lock.

Hull front area details. Another view shows the newly fabricated periscope covers as well as all the proper water hose connections to the water reservoir which is located between the hull and the stowage box. The two distinctive driver's hatch grab handles, made from 10-thou brass wire, have been attached.

View from the front: here you can see the many modifications and additions the IDF made to the T-55 tank.

View from the front: a full view of this awesome vehicle:

Wheels and T-55 tracks

WWII Productions of Australia have produced resin replacement tracks for years and these are certainly one of their best. These light grey resin tracks are fully workable, which means that they are individually connected and every link is independent of each other. Cleaning up and assembly is no more than a couple of hours' work and the results are well worth the time and the money.

Painting is easy; just be careful with them because some links tend to sometimes come apart if handled too roughly.

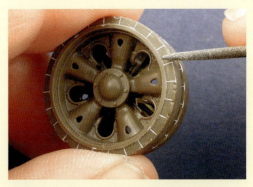

Carefully filing down the rubber edge of the kit T-55 starfish roadwheels with a small round file will give a worn effect. Also, I filled and sanded in the kit outer rubber ribbing effect which doesn't look realistic

My T-55 wheel-painting template comes into use. Simply cut the proper size hole onto 10-thou Evergreen styrene sheet and attach a tab for easy handling when painting.

WWII Productions' tracks are nothing short of amazing! After a couple of coats of Tamiya XF-69 Nato Black, for a worn look I apply my sponge chipping effects with Citadel Codex Grey acrylic paint.

The tracks are starting to look nice and dusty with the help of a custom mix of 'light earth' Holbein pastels as well as a number of 'dust' washes to give a nice effect.

The desert sand looks to be a red-brown colour. Here I apply a custom mix of Holbein pastel chalks to the inner wheel area.

committing to the final gluing. After painting and weathering the engine, I glued it into place, joined the upper and lower hulls together and started the painting and finishing.

Painting

Because of the different media used it's always good to give the model a dark primer coat that provides a constant medium for the base colour to adhere to. Heavily thinned Tamiya NATO Black is my choice for a good primer, and it seals the model perfectly using my Testors' Aztec airbrush. Perfection is not necessary here, though it is important to remember to get into all the corners and crevices and make sure the cream resin bits on the model are coated.

Before applying the NATO Black basecoat I added a bit of mud effects from my supply of ground-up pastel chalk. I simply dabbed a small amount of Tamiya thinner to the area then gently dropped the pastel chalk onto the area with a brush. This clumps up nicely and gives a nice mud-like effect to the lower hull area.

Since I was going to use a mixture of various dry transfers for the vehicle markings, I needed to mask off portions of the front fenders as well as turret areas. I wanted to paint the chevron recognition mark as well as the red ID front plate on the left-hand front fender.

It's an easy sequence: I just applied a number of thin coats of

After the usual pre-shade coating of Tamiya XF-69 Nato Black to the entire, vehicle I carefully masked off all areas where markings will be added. Here the white turret chevron marking as well as the white stripe that goes the length of the barrel are painted first with Vallejo Model Air 001 White and then carefully masked with a strip of Tamiya tape.

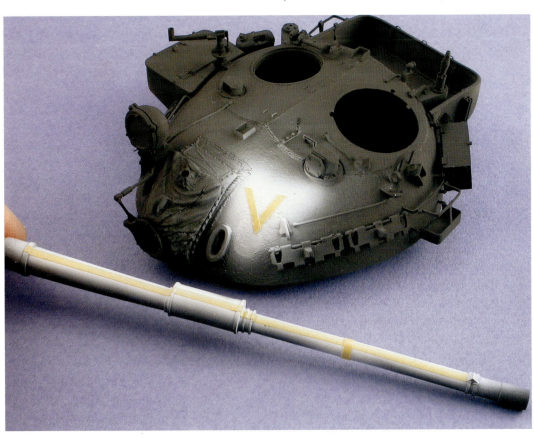

Applying the base coat: I carefully apply light coats of a mix of Vallejo Model Air to the turret with my Iwata Custom Micro airbrush. Note the Tamiya tape on the large side turret bin that will eventually have the proper markings once the basecoat is finally applied.

Vallejo White as well as Vallejo Red to the appropriate areas and then masked them with Tamiya tape. I then gentry burnished the taped areas to make sure no basecoat paint seeped in when applied later.

Since this vehicle is shown as a late variant the darker grey-green sand colour was needed for the scheme. After some careful research I decided to use the 'Lebanon 1980' mix of Vallejo Model Air Acrylics (three equal parts of 011 Tank Green, 049 Medium Sea Green and 055 Grey Green) as a close match to the Israeli sand colour I was looking for. With my trusty Iwata Custom Micro airbrush I carefully sprayed on the base colour in random patches until the colour was even throughout.

Applying the chips with a sponge: it looks awful now, but will start looking good with another coating of base colour.

I think it's a good idea to paint the turret and the main body separately, mainly because of all the delicate turret detail that may get damaged in the process.

Sponging on the chips

I've been using a make-up sponge to apply delicate chipping for worn effects for quite some time now. It's relatively simple to achieve to get all kinds of contrasts and effects in colour depending how you apply the paint to the model.

After the main base sand colour was done, I carefully applied small portions of Citadel Colour Black Ink, which is nice and thin right out of the bottle, to areas where chipping is needed. Don't worry if things look a bit overdone. The key here is to spray a thinned coating of the original base sand colour over the sponged areas; the idea here is to blend in the 'chips' so that an illusion of wear and tear results.

ABOVE Carefully applying Citadel Gunbolt Metal to the tow cable. Note the subtle chipping effect on the fuel tank.

After carefully removing all the Tamiya tape, the dry transfer markings can be applied and then sealed with a flat coat for protection. After applying a dark wash to the entire model, I went back with a clean brush with a bit of fresh turpentine to clean up the excess wash. Note the large turret bin now has the markings thanks to MIG Productions' dry transfers.

Markings

Finding the appropriate markings for this vehicle was a bit difficult. Luckily, Gilles Peiffer of Blast Models was kind enough to send me some nice shots of a late Tiran which clearly showed all the markings I needed.

What I can surmise from reading Michael Mass's excellent *Verlinden Warmachines 10* is that the single white band around the gun barrel indicates that this Tiran belonged to a first battalion of an armoured brigade; the white turret chevron indicates the company; and the white '1' in a red rectangle on the right front fender indicates the second tank of the first platoon.

Some quick improvisation was needed to finally get the markings together, so a combination of MIG Productions and Verlinden dry transfer sets were used with pretty good results.

To seal and protect the markings from subsequent washes, a quick coating of Vallejo 59 Matte Varnish was sprayed on to these areas. At this point, I painted the tow hooks as well as the tow shackles with Vallejo 861 Glossy Black, along with both jerrycans.

The inner engine hatches were painted Tamiya XF-7 Flat Red. Next, I went in once more with my Iwata and carefully began post-shading all the recessed and shaded areas of the vehicle, using a heavily thinned mix of Tamiya XF-1 Flat Black and XF-64 Red Brown, followed by a light 'wash' of a mix of Winsor & Newton Black and Burnt Sienna oil paints thinned with turpentine. Washes are easily applied with a thin brush, which not only gives depth to the overall look of the model but brings out the base colour.

Weathering

Instead of using a dark wash method of Winsor & Newton Black and Burnt Sienna, I made a

Applying the dust wash to the upper hull. Multiple applications were required to achieve the full effect.

The weathered dusty look starts to take shape. Note the front fenders now have their appropriate markings.

Applying a build-up of sand and dust with a mix of red-brown oil paint. The process takes a bit of practice and is time consuming but the results are pretty good.

custom blend of 'dust' using Winsor & Newton Naples Yellow and a touch of Raw Sienna. I thinned this with turpentine and carefully applied it using the regular thin Tamiya brush, dabbing the wash into crevices and places where dust would accumulate.

From a number of colour photos of this vehicle the fabric-covered mantlet, as well as the front glacis area, would see a large build-up of sand and dust accumulation. I started with a light dusting of a mixture of oils and added a couple of layers of dust to the front area. Afterwards I went back and applied a reddish-brown mix of raw sienna and yellow ochre oils, with which I tried to give the effect of sand and dust accumulation.

This effect was accomplished by just dabbing a small amount of wash onto the area; with repeated applications a build-up of colour occurs. Experiment on a scrap

References

Mass, Michael, *Warmachines No. 10: IDF T54, T-55, T-62* (Verlinden Publications: Belgium, 1991)

Model Detail Photo Monograph 9: T-55/55A Vol. 1 (Rossagraph: Warsaw)

Model Detail Photo Monograph 9: T-55/55A Vol. 2 (Rossagraph: Warsaw)

piece of plastic first. With a little patience some neat wash effects can be accomplished.

All that was left to do was to attach the two remaining 30mm turret machine guns and both turret antennae, which were made from 15- and 10-thou rod and stretched sprue.

SPECIAL THANKS

This project couldn't have happened without the kind help of fellow modellers:
Gilles Peiffer of Blast Models, who not only kindly supplied the resin update set for this build but was instrumental in helping with the markings and reference photos.
Bill Wiseman of WWII Productions, who graciously supplied a set of T-55 tracks.
Charlie Pritchett, who helped out with getting a VLS engine and whose constant help and inspiration will never be forgotten.
Chris Mrosko, who was so kind as to send me an assortment of rare Verlinden IDF detail items, which were instrumental in getting the details right.
And a special thanks to fellow modellers and IDF specialists: Michael Mass, Yehoshua Weingarten and Mark Hazzard for their kind help and insight.

References and research

If you want to make your model a replica of a specific original tank, or just to improve on what's in the kit, you'll need reference material. You can find this in all sorts of places, even on the television news or in newspapers if you build modern AFVs. But for most modellers these sources are not enough, simply because television gives a fleeting image and newspapers don't identify what they show you in a photograph. So let's look at where you can find the information you want. Magazines and the Allied–Axis series mentioned below have a spread of subjects – German, British, US, etc. Books, on the other hand, usually concentrate on the tanks of one nation so you need not buy the ones dealing with tanks that don't interest you.

Magazines

The first source for many modellers is the articles in magazines, so I'll start with those published in the UK. *Military Modelling* includes many articles by well-known and respected authors, both about building model tanks and about tank history as well as other military modelling subjects; it also includes reviews of new kits and books. It is available at most good newsagents. *AFV Modeller* is also very good, with building articles and reviews, and has a detailed photographic section on a particular tank or weapon in almost every issue, but is only sold by subscription or if the company has a stand at a model show. *Model Military International* is a specialist military modelling magazine from the same publishers as *Tamiya Model Magazine International* (see below) with a lot of tank-modelling articles. Like its stablemate it can be found in large newsagents. *Tamiya Model Magazine International*, *Military Modelcraft* and *Scale Models International* also have AFV modelling articles, though you may not find them in your newsagent so easily, and they do have articles about other kinds of models.

From the US there is one dedicated tank modelling magazine, *Military Miniatures in Review*. It is published quarterly, though not always on time, and has very good modelling articles. UK readers can get it from Historex Agents (see the following chapter). MMiR has a sister publication, *Allied–Axis*, devoted to detailed photographs of a few tanks or AFVs in each issue and also available from Historex Agents. Both of these are very well worth getting. The US also offers *FineScale Modeler*, which, as its title suggests, covers all kinds of models. You can find it in larger newsagents but it often has no tank-related content.

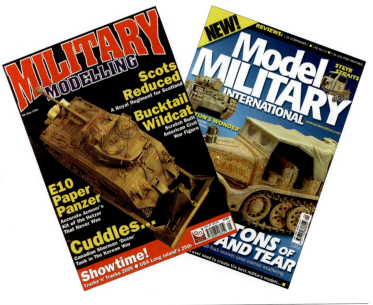

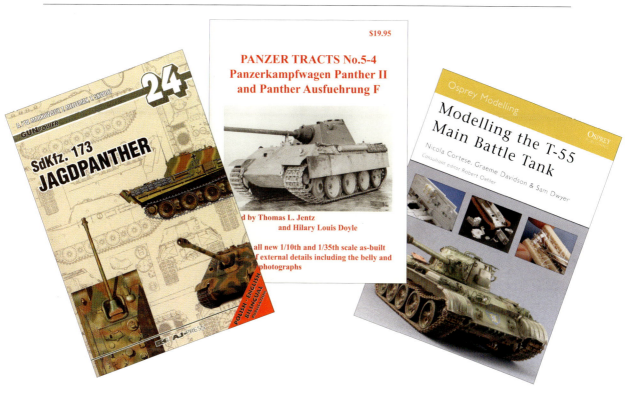

Among non-English-language magazines there is *Steelmasters* from France. It is easy enough to read with 'schoolboy French' and has many interesting articles. *Xtreme Modelling* is bilingual English/Spanish and, although I cannot comment on it because I have not seen it, it is highly recommended by those who have. Japanese magazines have highly detailed articles about tank modelling, sometimes with English captions to their photographs; Model Graphix offers a range of books as well as *Armor Modelling* magazine, Sunday Art has *Panzer* magazine, and the Ground Power series of books contains some very good reference photographs. Even though they're in Japanese these are all worth looking at.

Books

Now let's look at books about tanks and armoured fighting vehicles. The Osprey New Vanguard series is always a good start, covering many different tanks from various nations and periods at a low price. If you find any of the older Osprey Vanguard series, now out of print, you'll discover that it includes books on tanks that have not yet been included in New Vanguards. Both series are very useful indeed, written by highly authoritative authors and with text, photographs and colour plates that will give you plenty of information and ideas for your models.

Ian Allan also has two low-priced series of books about tanks, Tanks in Detail and Tanks and Armour. These have more text and, apart from the first two books in the Tanks in Detail series, are also very useful.

A third publisher is Concord, with several series of low-priced books about tanks. These have little text but many photographs as well as colour plates, all with detailed captions.

Squadron-Signal is another low-priced publisher with several book series about tanks. They come between the Osprey and Ian Allan series and those from Concord, with more text to describe the tanks as well as plenty of photographs. Most of them also have colour plates.

If your interest is German tanks you really must buy the Panzer Tracts book series by Thomas Jentz and Hilary Louis Doyle. These are meticulously researched from original German archives and cover their subjects in great detail with text, plans and rare photographs all at reasonable prices. This is probably the most highly respected source for information about and plans of German World War II tanks. Equally great references for German armour is the Nuts & Bolts series, with plenty of detailed photographs of preserved vehicles; the later volumes also have a very detailed text, plans, colour plates and many photographs of the vehicles in service. These two series are exceptional value and complement each other, so don't think you should only buy from one series. Both are available from military booksellers or direct from the publishers.

There are also quite a few out-of-print books from other publishers that are useful if you can find them. Verlinden Publications' series War Machines gives detailed coverage of specific tanks and armoured vehicles, with all photographs in colour and detailed captions. Arms & Armour Press had two series, Tanks Illustrated and Military Vehicles Fotofax. The first ran to over 20 books, dealing with tanks and AFVs from many nations at many periods, and was full of period photographs. The second only had four books, but was equally full of period photographs and also included plans of its subjects. Darlington Publications had a series called Museum Ordnance Specials, very well worth buying if you see them, with detailed photographic coverage of particular vehicles from World War II to the 1980s.

French tanks and AFVs are very well dealt with in a series of books from Trackstory of France, with bilingual English/French text and

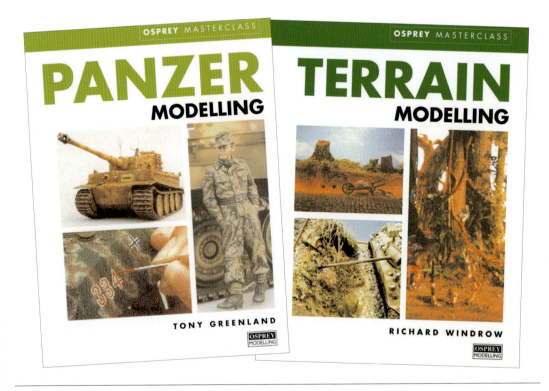

many rare photographs. The first one is already out of print as I write, so if you are interested in French tanks and spot one of the Trackstory titles buy it straight away!

Publications MBI of the Czech Republic and AJ Press of Poland also have reasonably priced books. MBI concentrates on Czech-built World War II tanks and AFVs such as the Panzer 35 and Panzer 38 and their derivates like the Hetzer, while AJ Press has good books about several German tanks as well as being the only English-language publisher of books about Japanese tanks. Both these publishers give detailed plans and many photographs as well as good text, in many cases bilingual so you can learn the Czech and Polish terms to help if you pick up a book about tanks in either language.

British tanks, alas, only feature at low prices in the Osprey series mentioned above.

All of these are relatively cheap and form the basis of a good private library. Between them they cover most of the significant tanks of World War II and many more modern ones as well.

Looking now at the more expensive books, if your interest is US-built tanks and AFVs there is a whole series by R. P. Hunnicutt covering everything built in the US from World War I to their dates of publication. They came out a long time ago, so the most modern

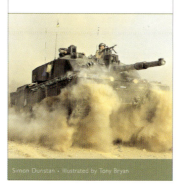

AFVs are not included, though the Abrams is featured. Most of them are out of print and very expensive if you find a second-hand copy, but some are still available from military bookshops as new books. They are regarded as 'the Bible' for anyone interested in American tanks, particularly in Shermans and Stuarts.

For anyone interested in German tanks there are several series of books. Walter Spielberger's series for Motorbuch Verlag of Germany dealt in separate volumes with everything from the Panzer I to the Leopard I in great detail. Unfortunately only a few of them were translated into English, but even those only available in German are superb references and can be puzzled through with the help of a German–English dictionary. They are now out of print and fetch high prices as second-hand books, but like the Hunnicutt books they

are worth paying for. Schiffer Books also has some excellent volumes about German tanks, particularly the Panther and Tiger where the noted expert Thomas Jentz has written multi-book sets.

The most detailed English-language books about Russian tanks are those by Steven Zaloga for several publishers. Osprey publishes some of them and Ian Allan has a series in English by the respected Russian author Mikhail Baryatinsky, so they're not all at the expensive end of the market! Unfortunately most of the Russian-language books have not yet been translated, but if you see one in Russian it will be worth getting for its photographs found in Russian archives – it's not too hard to work out which Cyrillic letters mean T-34, IS-2, etc!

Histoire & Collections of France has several books dealing with French Army armoured units and other World War II subjects. Don't be deceived by the Napoleonic-period figures on the covers of some of them; take a look inside to see whether they deal with tanks too. 'Schoolboy French' will get you through the photograph captions and most of the text of the ones that are not available in English translations.

The best books about British tanks of World War II are those written by David Fletcher. Some are in the pricey range, but he has also written Osprey New

Vanguards. If you see his out-of-print books for HMSO about the Churchill and Cromwell tanks, seize them immediately!

INTERNET RESOURCES

The Internet is becoming increasingly useful as a resource for tank modellers, with some very good dedicated discussion groups. If you visit any of them with a question, do make sure that you use the search facilities provided by some before asking a question that may have been answered many times before! Missing Links (http://www.missing-lynx.com/) and Track-Link (http://www.track-link.net/) have the best English-language discussion groups for modellers as well as kit, accessory and book reviews together with galleries of readers' model photographs. The Perth Military Modelling Site (http://www.perthmilitarymodelling.com/), known to everyone as PMMS, is probably the best site you'll ever find specializing in reviews and is usually the first to post reviews of new kits. Both Missing Links and Track-Link are great sources of advice, with very knowledgeable modellers happy to share their expertise, and modellers also post to the AFV News discussion group at http://www.comcentral.net/index.php?name=Forums&file=viewforum&f=73, which is also

frequented by tank crewmen and other people interested in real AFVs. There are also quite a few discussion groups on Yahoo (http://groups.yahoo.com) for those interested in specific tanks or armies – Sherman, Stuart, M8 Greyhound armoured cars and Japanese armour, to name just four. Many discussion groups require registration before you can post messages, but this is not a difficult process and it does keep spammers away.

Check Tony Matteliano's Scale Model Index website (http://www.scalemodelindex.com/) for a host of other discussion groups, manufacturers' and retailers' websites, references websites, museum websites and model society web addresses.

MUSEUMS

And speaking of museum websites, there is no substitute for seeing the real thing, so make a point of visiting any armour museum you can reach. In the UK there are the Tank Museum, Bovington (http://www.tankmuseum.co.uk/, telephone +44 (0)1929 405096, postal address Bovington, Dorset, BH20 6JG), with its superb collection of tanks and equally superb reference and photograph libraries (you need to make an appointment to visit the libraries) and the Land Warfare Hall at the Imperial War Museum's Duxford Annex (http://www.iwm.org.uk/,

email duxford@iwm.org.uk, telephone +44 (0)1223 835 000, postal address Duxford, Cambridgeshire, CB2 4QR), which is also fascinating although its collection is smaller. The main building of the Imperial War Museum in London (email mail@iwm.org.uk, telephone +44 (0)207 416 5320, postal address Lambeth Road, London SE1 6HZ) has a massive photograph archive too, but again you must make an appointment to visit it.

Smaller, but still well worth a visit, are the Muckleburgh Collection (http://www.muckleburgh.co.uk/home.htm, telephone +44 (0)1263 588210, postal address Weybourne, Norfolk) and the Cobbaton Combat Collection (http://www.cobbatoncombat.co.uk/, email info@cobbatoncombat.co.uk, telephone +44 (0)1769 540740, postal address Chittlehampton, Umberleigh, North Devon, EX37 9RZ).

In Europe there are more splendid armour collections in the Musée des Blindés at Saumur (http://www.musee-des-blindes.asso.fr/, email museedesblindes@wanadoo.fr, telephone +33 (0)2 41 83 69 95, postal address 1043, route de Fontevraud, 49400 – Saumur, France). Germany has the Panzer Museum in Munster (http://www.munster.de/pzm/, email panzermuseum@munster.de, telephone +49 (0)5192 130240, postal address Hans-Krüger Straße 33, 29633 Munster), the Wehrtechnische Studiensammlung at Koblenz (http://www.bwb. org/C1256DF2004FF94C/Docna me/ORGANISATION_WTS_IN DEX.HTM, email WTS@BWB. ORG, telephone +49 (0)261 400 1423, postal address Mayener Strasse 85-87, 56070 Koblenz), the Militärhistorisches Museum der Bundeswehr in Dresden (email MilHistMuseumBWEingang@Bun deswehr.ORG, telephone +49 (0)351 8232803, postal address Olbrichtplatz 2, 01099 Dresden), and the Auto & Technik Museum near Frankfurt (http://www. technik-museum.de/uk/sinsheim/, telephone +49 (0)7261 9299 0, postal address Museumsplatz, D-74889 Sinsheim). Sweden has the Pansarmuseet at Axvall (http://www.pansarmuseet.se/, email info@pansarmuseet.se, postal address Pansarmuseet, Tekniska enheten by 25, Box 604, 541 29 Skövde), and in Russia there is the famous museum at Kubinka (http://www.tank museum.ru/) where access is restricted because it is on a military base. To visit there either go on an organized specialized tour or follow the instructions on the website for permission.

North America, of course, has a host of military museums – far too many to list here. The Scale Model Index has links to the websites of many of those that are open to the public, but some are private so you need to be introduced by someone already known there.

OTHER RESOURCES

Wherever you live there will be a military vehicle collector somewhere near you. Go to the open days at Bovington and Duxford or to the annual War and Peace Show at Beltring near Maidstone (http://www. thewarandpeaceshow.com/) and you'll find hordes of tanks, trucks and artillery whose owners are usually very happy to let you photograph their vehicles. Readers in other countries will find just as many shows in their areas, and owners just as happy to show off their collections. Take a camera and plenty of film, or memory cards, and you can have a good collection of reference photographs. Don't miss the opportunity to ask about joining a preservation society in your area; membership fees are usually low and you don't have to own a tank to join.

You can also join your local model club, or a national or international one – the International Plastic Modellers Society (http://www.ipms-uk.co.uk/) and Armour Modelling & Preservation Society (http:// www.amps-armor.org/) both have local groups in many countries, and have Internet discussion groups for tank modellers as well as society magazines.

And finally, when you see an AFV in a museum or at a show always remember that restorations are rarely perfect. The most dedicated collectors go to enormous lengths to find original parts and even to make copies of original parts lent to them, and some vehicles remained in service so long that restorations are perfect apart from changes needed to meet modern laws. The direction indicators on preserved Jeeps are a typical example: wartime vehicles did not have winking indicators! Their owners will tell you what is not an original fitting, so make a note and don't copy those features in your models. Museums do not usually have that much money to spend, so their exhibits may have missing parts or be restored wrongly to help preserve them. This can mean that a 'wrong' headlamp has been installed instead of a gap being left where it should be, or that a fictitious colour scheme has been applied when the vehicle absolutely had to be repainted to stop it rusting. A very few museum exhibits are known to have been rebuilt on salvaged chassis as the restorer's best guess at the original appearance, but fortunately you won't meet many like that. Compare what you have seen and photographed with photographs of the wartime tanks and you'll soon see what to ignore when you build your models!

SOURCES

It would be impossible to list all the sources of kits, accessories, magazines and books in a book this size, but I have included all those mentioned in the earlier chapters and as many manufacturers and good shops as possible. The listings are in alphabetical order. Some of the firms deal only on the internet so have no postal addresses or telephone numbers. All telephone numbers have been given as if dialled internationally.

KIT AND ACCESSORY MAKERS

Aber (maker of etched-metal sets)
40 060 Katowice, ul. Fliegera 16, Poland
http://www.aber.net.pl/
Email contact@aber.net.pl
Tel +48 (0)32 203 24 05
Fax +48 (0)32 608 69 81

Accurate Armour (maker of multimedia kits and UK importer of several ranges)
Units 13–16, Kingston Industrial Estate, Port Glasgow, Inverclyde, PA14 5DG, UK
http://www.accurate-armour.com/
Email info@accurate-armour.com
Tel +44 (0)1475 743955
Fax +44 (0)1475 743746

Airedale Castings (maker of a few very good resin kits and conversions)
http://airedalecastings.mysite.wanadoo-members.co.uk/
Email airedalecastings@hotmail.com

Archer Fine Transfers (maker of excellent rub-down decals in several scales)
PO Box 1277, Youngsville, NC 27596-1277, USA
http://www.archertransfers.com/
Email info@archertransfers.com
Tel +1 919 570 1026

Armorscale (maker of turned metal gun barrels and other accessories)
Grabowski Robert, ul. Dmowskiego 21/116, 43-100 Tychy, Poland
http://www.armorscale.com/#
Email info@armorscale.com
Fax +48 (0)32 328 36 84

Azimut Productions (maker of resin kits and conversions and accessories)
113 Rue de Turenne, 75003 Paris, France
http://www.azimutproductions.com/
Email azimutproductions@cegetel.net
Tel +33 (0)1 44 59 33 44
Fax +33 (0)1 44 59 33 48

Baluard Models (maker of 1/35-scale railway locos, etc.)
c/o Rector Bruguera, 28, bj., 08003 Barcelona, Spain
http://www.baluardmodels.com/
Email info@baluardmodels.com
Tel/fax: +34 93 221 18 93

Bison Decals (maker of waterslide decals in several scales)
http://www.angelfire.com/pro/bison/
Email bison_decals@lycos.com

Blast Models (maker of resin conversions and also retailers of several ranges)
5 rue Crozatier, 75012 Paris, France
http://www.phpshopxml.com/blamod.shop/
Email info@blast-models.com;
Tel +33 (0)1 43 46 00 66
Fax +33 (0)1 43 46 00 50

Calibre 35 (maker of resin items in several scales)
http://www.calibre35.cz/
Email info@calibre35.cz

CMK (maker of resin kits and detail sets)
Mezilesi 718, 193 00 Praha 9, Czech Republic
http://www.cmkkits.com/
Tel +420 2 819 23909
Fax +420 2 819 23910

Crielmodel (maker of resin kits)
Cristiana Cerruti, via della Giustiniana, 50 00188 Rome, Italy
http://crielmodel.it/
Tel +39 06 39376254
Fax +39 06 39376254

Cromwell Models (maker of resin kits and conversions)
6/6 The Quadrangle, 57 Ruchill Street, Glasgow, G20 9PX, Scotland, UK
http://www.xs4all.nl/~cromwell/
Email cromwellmodels@yahoo.co.uk;
Tel +44 (0)141 948 0255
Tel +44 (0)141 942 8596
Fax +44 (0)141 948 0236

Decalcomaniacs! (maker of waterslide decals)
http://www.decalcomaniacs.net/

Des Kit (maker of resin kits)
27 Rue des Hauts de Bonne Eau, 94 500 Champigny sur Marne, France
http://deskit.online.fr/
Tel/fax +33 (0)1 48 81 58 67

Dragon Models (maker of polystyrene kits)
B1-10/F., 603-609 Castle Peak Road., Kong Nam Industrial Building, Tsuen Wan, N. T., Hong Kong
http://www.dragon-models.com/
Tel +852 2493 0215
Fax +852 2411 0587

Dragon Models USA, Inc (importers)
1315 John Reed Court, City of Industry, CA 91745, USA
http://www.dragonmodelsusa.com/
Email sales@dragonmodelsusa.com
Tel +1 626 968 0322
Fax +1 626 968 0234

Echelon Fine Details (maker of waterslide decals)
http://pachome1.pacific.net.sg/~kriegsketten/
Email kriegsketten@pacific.net.sg

Eduard Model Accessories (maker of etched-metal sets and some kits)
Mírová 170, 43521 Obrnice, Czech Republic
http://www.eduard.cz/
Email department@eduard.cz
Tel +420 476 118668
Tel +420 476 118259
Fax +420 476 118171

Fingerprint Designs (maker of waterslide decals)
Belmont House, 22 Kent Road, Southport, Merseyside, PR8 4BJ, UK
http://www.fingerprintdesigns.supanet.com/
Email fingerprintdesigns@supanet.com

Firing Line (maker of multimedia kits in several scales)
David J Parkins, Trefacwn Fach, Llanrhian, St. Davids, Pembrokeshire, SA62 6DP, Wales, UK
http://www.djparkins.clara.net/fline/flmaster.htm
Email djparkins@aol.com
Tel +44 (0)1348 831887
Fax +44 (0)1348 837542

Formations Models (maker of resin kits and conversions)
PO Box 424, Bolivar, TN 38008-0424, USA
http://www.formationsmodels.com/
Email info@formationsmodels.com
Tel +1 731 658 1521

Friulmodel (maker of white-metal tracks)
8142 Urhida, Nefelejcs u. 2, Hungary
http://www.friulmodel.hu/
Email friulmodel@matavnet.hu

Great North Roads (maker of scenic bases and buildings)
http://www.greatnorthroads.co.uk/
Email s.farrugia@ntlworld.com
Tel +44 (0)2392 366722

Hansa Systems USA (maker of polystyrene parts to construct your own buildings)
8 South Meadow Glen Road, Kings Park, NY 11754, USA
http://www.hansasystemsusa.com/
Email peter@hansasystemsusa.com
Tel +1 631 269 9067
Fax +1 631 269 9143

Hard Corps Models (maker of resin figures, rubdown decals and book publisher)
551 Wheeler Drive, Moscow Mills, MO 63362, USA
http://hardcorpsmodels.com/

Heller SA (maker of polystyrene kits)
B.P. 5, 61160 Trun, France
http://www.heller.fr

Hornet & Wolf (maker of figure kits in resin and white metal)
Roger Saunders, 290 Queen's Road, London, SE14 5JN, UK
http://www.greenwichgateway.com/hornetandwolf/
Email hornetandwolf@hotmail.com
Tel/fax +44 (0)20 7639 9409

Humbrol Ltd (maker of paints and of Airfix polystyrene kits)
Marfleet, Hull, HU9 5NE, UK
http://airfix.com/
Email airfixservices@humbrol.com
Tel +44 (0)1482 701191

Italeri spa (maker of polystyrene kits)
Via Pradazzo 6/B, 40012 Calderare di Reno BO, Italy
http://www.italeri.com/
Tel +39 051 726037
Fax +39 051 726459

Italian Kits (maker of resin kits and retailer of many Italian ranges)
PO Box 115-20092 Cinisello B. (MI), Italy
http://www.italiankits.it/ineng.html
Email info@italiankits.com

Jadar-Model (maker of multimedia kits and retailer of many Polish ranges)
Zielna 8 Street, Shop 103, 00-108 Warsaw, Poland
http://www.jadar.com.pl/
Email hobby@jadarhobby.waw.pl

Japanese Armor King (maker of resin kits of Japanese tanks and figures)
Ted Dyer Inc., PO Box 1030, Roslyn, PA 19001-9030, USA
http://www.japanesearmorking.com/
Email DyersArt@Comcast.Net

K59 (maker of resin upgrade sets)
http://www.k59.hk/
Email k59@netvigator.com

Legend Productions (maker of resin kits, conversions and figures)
Seokwang Building 202, Sukchon-Dong 282-2, Songpa-Gu, Seoul, Korea
http://www.www-legend.co.kr/main.htm
Email swimsarang@korea.com
Tel +82 2 414 0129
Fax +82 2 414 0145

Lion Roar Art Model Co (maker of etched-metal sets)
708 Changle Road, Shanghai, China, 200040
http://www.lionroar.net/
Tel/fax +86 21 54038638

MIG Productions (maker of pigment powders and resin accessories)
http://www.migproductions.com/
Email info@migproductions.com
Tel/fax +34 948 555 772

Milicast Model Company (maker of small-scale kits)
9 Rannoch Street, Battlefield, Glasgow, G44 4DF, Scotland, UK
http://www.milicast.com/
Email milicastmodels@hotmail.com
Tel +44 (0)141 633 1400

Mission Models (maker of tools for working with etched metal and kit retailer)
215 W. Palm Ave No.103, Burbank , California, 91502, USA
http://www.missionmodels.com
Email info@missionmodels.com
Tel +1 818 842 1885
Fax +1 818 842 1886

MK35 Editions (maker of resin figures and accessories)
Chemin des Esperettes, 30200 Saint-Laurent de Carnols, France
http://perso.wanadoo.fr/mk35.editions/index.html
Email mk35.editionsr@wanadoo.fr
Tel +33 (0)466 827 041
Fax +33 (0)466 827 095

Modelling Artisan Mori (maker of resin figures and accessories)
http://www3.ocn.ne.jp/~m.a.mori/
Email m.a.mori@wonder.ocn.ne.jp

Model Point US, LLC (maker of turned metal gun barrels and multimedia upgrades and accessories)
PO Box 114132, North Providence, RI 02911, USA
http://www.modelpoint.us/
Email info@modelpoint.us

Monroe Perdu Studios (maker of resin and card parts for bases)
3168 Renee Court, Simi Valley, CA 93065, USA
http://www.monroeperdu.com/
Email sales@monroeperdu.com

Moskit Tech (maker of pre-rusted exhaust pipes)
http://www.moskittech.ru/eng/glav.php

Mouse House Enterprises (maker of decals and resin conversions)
PO Box 9112, Deakin, ACT 2600, Australia
http://mheaust.com.au/MHE/MHEmain.htm
Email info@mheaust.com.au;
Tel (evenings only) +61 (0)2 4844 6271
Fax +61 (0)2 4844 6248

MR Modelbau (maker of resin kits and conversions)
MR Modellbau Matthias Roth, Adalbertstraße 7a, D-38690 Vienenburg, Germany
http://www.mrmodellbau.de/
Email MRModellbau@t-online.de
Tel +49 (0)5324 798318
Fax +49 (0)5324 69733

New Connection Models (maker of resin kits and conversions)
Dorfgütingen 40, 91555 Feuchtwangen, Germany
http://www.new-connection.de/
Tel +49 (0)9852 4329
Fax +49 (0)9852 2804

Nimix (maker of resin and etched-metal kits, accessories and figures)
Apartado de Correos 45.117,Madrid 28080, Spain
http://www.nimix.net/
Email pedidos@nimix.net
Tel/fax +34 352 81 39

Plus Model Ltd (maker of resin and multimedia kits and accessories)
Jizní 56, 370 10 Ceské Budejovice, Czech Republic
http://www.plusmodel.cz
Email plusmodel@plusmodel.cz
Tel/fax +420 387 220 111

Precision Models (maker of resin kits, accessories and figures)
Elf-Septemberlaan 24, 3660 Opglabbeek, Belgium
http://www.ping.be/~p4u00782/Index.htm
Email precisionmodels@ping.be
Tel +32 (0)89 85 30 34
Fax +32 (0)89 85 83 22

Quartermaster's Depot (maker of decals and printed paper items)
http://store.quartermastersdepot.com/

R&J Enterprises (maker of resin conversion and detailing parts and retailers of many ranges)
PO Box 39, Quilcene, WA 98376-0039, USA
http://www.rjproducts.com/
Email rj@rjproducts.com
Tel/fax +1 360 796 3828

Real Model (maker of resin kits, conversions and accessories)
http://www.realmodel.cz/
Email info@realmodel.cz

Resicast (maker of resin kits, conversions and figures)
http://www.resicast.com/
Email infos@resicast.com

Revell GmbH & Co KG (maker of polystyrene kits)
Henschelstraße 20-30, D-32257 Bünde, Germany
http://www.revell.de/de/
Email contact_d@revell.de
Tel +49 (0)5223 9650
Fax +49 (0)5223 965488

Royal Model (maker of resin and etched-metal upgrade sets)
http://www.royalmodel.com/
Email customerscare@royalmodel.com

Scale Link Ltd (maker of white-metal and etched-metal kits and accessories, and retailers of many ranges)
Farrington, Dorset, DT11 8RA, UK
http://www.scalelink.co.uk/
Email info@scalelink.co.uk
Tel/fax +44 (0)1747 811817

Schatton Modellbau (maker of turned metal gun barrels and ammunition
Industriestrasse 6, 94347 Ascha, Germany
http://www.modellbau-schatton.privat.t-online.de/index.html
Email modellbau.schatton@t-online.de
Tel +49 (0)9961 6246 and 6409
Fax +49 (0)9961 9107826

The Small Shop EU (maker of tools for working with etched metal)
4 Woodpecker Meadow, Gillingham, Dorset, SP8 4GB, UK
http://www.thesmallshopeu.com
Email info@thesmallshopeu.com
Tel/fax +44 (0)1747 825646

Tamiya, Inc (maker of polystyrene kits)
3–7 Ondawara, Shizuoka City, Japan
http://tamiya.com/

Tank (maker of resin figures and accessories)
http://www.tank-model.ru/
Email Contact@tank-model.ru

Tank WorkShop (maker of resin kits, conversions and accessories)
345 Wynbrook Dr, McDonough, GA 30253, USA
http://www.tankworkshop.com/
Email info@tankworkshop.com
Tel +1 770 573 1409
Fax +1 770 573 0479

Tiger Model Designs (maker of resin kits, conversions and accessories)
5305 B Bertha Nelson Road, Panama City, FL 32404-9113, USA
http://www.tigermodels.com/
Email info@tigermodels.com
Tel +1 850 763 2529
Fax +1 850 522 6474

VLS Corporation (maker of several ranges of resin kits and major retailer)
1011 Industrial Court. Moscow Mills, MO 63362, USA
http://www.modelmecca.com/
Email sales@modelmecca.com
Tel +1 636 356 4888
Fax +1 636 356 4877

White Ensign Models (maker of paints for armour models)
South Farm, Snitton, Ludlow, SY8 3EZ, UK
http://www.whiteensignmodels.com/
Email wem@onetel.com
Tel +44 (0)870 220 1888
Fax +44 (0)870 220 1786

MAIL-ORDER SHOPS

These are shops that I have dealt with and can recommend. I have not duplicated the entries above for retailers who also make or import kits and other items.

AFV Modeller Shop (UK importer of several ranges)
AFV Modeller Ltd, 176 New Bridge Street, Newcastle, Tyne & Wear, NE1 2TE, UK
http://shop.afvmodeller.com/customer/home.php
Tel +44 (0)191 209 117
Fax +44 (0)191 209 2002

F&S Scale Models
227 Droylsden Road, Audenshaw, Manchester, M34 5ZT, UK
http://www.fandsscalemodels.co.uk/
Email sales@fandsscalemodels.co.uk
Tel +44 (0)161 370 3235;
Fax +44 (0)161 370 3235

Hannants
H G Hannant Ltd, Harbour Road, Oulton Broad, Lowestoft, Suffolk, NR32 3LZ, UK
Also Hannants London at Unit 2, Hurricane Industrial Estate, Avion Crescent, Grahame Park Way, Colindale, London, NW9 5QW , UK
http://www.hannants.co.uk/
Email sales@hannants.co.uk
Tel +44 (0)1502 517444 or (0)845 130 72 48

Historex Agents (UK importer of many ranges)
Wellington House, 157 Snargate Street, Dover, Kent, CT17 9BZ, UK
http://www.historexagents.com/
Email sales@historex-agents.co.uk
Tel +44 (0)1304 206720

Hobbyeasy
Room 1805, Phase 2, Chai Wan Industrial City, 70 Wing Tai Road, Chai Wan, Hong Kong
http://www.hobbyeasy.com/Home.do?status=yes
Email info@hobbyeasy.com
Fax +852 2172 4355

Hobbylink Japan
Tatebayashi-shi, Nishitakane-cho 43-6, Gunma 374-0075, Japan
http://www.hlj.com/
Fax +81 276 80 3067

LSA Models
151 Sackville Road, Hove, East Sussex, BN3 3HD, UK
Email orders@lsamodels.co.uk
Tel/fax +44 (0)1273 705420

M&Models
9329 S. Cicero Avenue, Oak Lawn, IL 60453, USA
http://www.home.earthlink.net/~mmodels/
Email mmodels@earthlink.net
Tel/fax +1 708 423 7202

Martola Model Shop
ul. Sklep Modelarski Martola, AD MEDIA Sp. z o.o., od 16.12 - ul.Kielecka 40, Warsaw, Poland
http://www.martola.com.pl/index.php?lang=en
Email martola@martola.com.pl
Tel +48 (0)602 609669
Fax +48 (0)22 6654020

NKR Models
PO Box 25, Linton, Victoria 3360, Australia
http://www.nkrmodels.com.au/
Email NKRModel@netconnect.com.au
Tel/fax +61 (0)3 5344 7699

Rainbow Ten Co Ltd
623-1, Ikeda, Shizuoka-City, Suruga-ku, Shizuoka-Pref,
422-8005, Japan
http://www.rainbowten.co.jp/
Email info@rainbowten.co.jp
Fax +81 54655 1988

Squadron
Squadron Mail Order, 1115 Crowley Drive, Carrollton,
TX 75011-5010, USA
http://www.squadron.com/
Email mailorder@squadron.com;
Tel +1 972 242 8663l
Fax +1 972 242 3775

BOOKSHOPS AND PUBLISHERS

Reference books can be bought through military
bookshops, good mail-order hobby shops or even
mainstream bookshops if they take orders, and most of
the magazines are available from newsagents, so I'll
confine this section to those with websites in English or
with an English-language option. Most of the book
publishers listed offer direct sales.

ADH Publishing (*Tamiya Model Magazine International* and
Model Military International)
ADH Publishing Ltd, Doolittle Mill, Doolittle Lane,
Totternhoe, Beds, LU6 1QX, UK
http://www.tamiyamodelmagazine.com/
Email modmagint@aol.com
Tel +44 (0)1525 222573
Fax +44 (0)1525 222574

AFV Modeller magazine (subscription details)
http://www.afvmodeller.com/
Subscription link from website.

AJ Press (bilingual English/Polish books on
tanks of several nations)
http://aj-press.home.pl/main_euro.htm

Amazon (a good source for many books)
http://www.amazon.co.uk and www.amazon.com

Ampersand Publishing Co, Inc (*Military Miniatures in
Review*, Allied–Axis and books)
235 NE 6th Avenue, Suite G, Delray Beach, FL 33483,
USA
http://www.ampersandpublishing.com
Email Patmmir@aol.com
Tel +1 561 266 9686

Australian Military Equipment Profiles (useful
booklets on equipment used in Australia)
Michael Cecil, 'Linton', 560 Collector Road, Gunning,
NSW , Australia, 2581
http://www.users.bigpond.com/AMEP/index.html
Email amep@bigpond.com

Barbarossa Books (mail-order bookshop and publisher)
14 Maldon Road, Tiptree, Essex, CO5 0LL, UK
http://www.barbarossabooks.co.uk/
Email sales@barbarossabooks.co.uk
Tel +44 (0)1621 810 810
Fax +44 (0)1621 810 888

Concord Publications Company (several series of
books on AFVs)
http://www.concord-publications.com/

Czech-Six Publications (UK importer of books from
Publications MBI)
17 Goodwyns Place, Tower Hill, Dorking, Surrey, RH4
2AW , UK
http://www.czechsixpublications.com/
Email markt135-csp@yahoo.co.uk
Tel +44 (0)1306 889584

George R Bradford (publisher of 1/35- and 1/48-scale
plans)
10 Brenda Street RR.32 , Cambridge, Ontario, Canada,
N3H 4R7
http://www.afvnews.ca/
Email gbradford@sympatico.ca

Histoire et Collections (publisher of *Steelmasters*
magazine and several series of books)
http://www.histoireetcollections.com/

Ian Allan Publishing (publisher of books on AFVs and bookshop with other publishers' books)
http://www.ianallanpublishing.com/

JJ Fedorowicz Publishing Inc (publisher of books on AFVs and bookshop with other publishers' books)
104 Browning Boulevard, Winnipeg MB, R3K 0L7, Canada
http://www.jjfpub.mb.ca/
Email jjfpub@jjfpub.mb.ca
Tel +1 204 837 6080
Fax +1 204 889 1960

Kagero (publisher of books on AFVs including the Photosniper series)
Oficyna Wydawnicza KAGERO, ul. Melgiewska 7-9, 20-952 Lublin, Poland
http://www.kagero.pl/
Email kagero@kagero.kki.pl;
Tel/fax +48 81 759 6503

Military Modelling magazine
UK Subscriptions: Tower House, Sovereign Park, Market Harborough, Leicestershire, LE16 9EF
Email militarymodelling@subscription.co.uk
Tel +44 (0)870 8378600
North America subscriptions: Wise Owl Worldwide Publications, 5674 El Camino Real, Suite D, Carlsbad, CA 92008-7130, USA
www.wiseownmagazines.com
Email info@wiseowlmagazine.com
Tel +1 760 603 9768
Fax +1 760 603 9769

Osprey Publishing Ltd (publisher of New Vanguard books)
Osprey Direct, PO Box 140, Wellingborough, Northants, NN8 2FA, UK
http://www.ospreypublishing.com/
UK, Europe and rest of world email info@ospreydirect.co.uk
Canada and USA info@ospreydirect.com
UK, Europe and the rest of the world Tel +44 (0)1933 443 863, fax +44 (0)1933 443 849
Canada and USA tel toll free: +1 866 620 6941, fax +1 708 534 7803

Panzer Tracts (publisher of Panzer Tracts)
PO Box 334, Boyds, MD 20841-0334, USA
http://www.panzertracts.com
Tel/fax +1 301 972 2504

Schiffer Books (publisher of books on AFVs)
4880 Lower Valley Road., Atglen, PA 19310, USA
http://www.schifferbooks.com/
Email info@schifferbooks.com
Tel +1 610 593 1777
Fax +1 610 593 2002

Sentinel (publisher of books on Australian AFVs)
PO Box 9112, Deakin, ACT 2600, Australia
http://mheaust.com.au
Email info@mheaust.com.au
Tel +61 (0)2 4844 6271
Fax +61 (0)2 4844 6248

Trackstory (publisher of Trackstory bilingual English/French books on French AFVs)
25 rue des Jardins, 91160 Ballainvilliers, France
http://perso.orange.fr/minitracks/
Email ed-barbotin@wanadoo.fr

SOURCES OF OUT-OF-PRINT BOOKS

Used military book dealers advertise in several modelling magazines and can often be found at military vehicle shows too. If you cannot find what you want in their stocks it is always worth trying these two online book-search websites, and also Amazon and its non-English language branches where used books can sometimes be found.
Abebooks – http://www.abebooks.com
Bookfinder – http://www.bookfinder.com

Index

A

accordions 59
acrylic paint 10, **10**, 113–14
adhesives *see* glues
aerials 69
AFV Modeller (magazine) 174
AFV News discussion group 178
air filters **83**
airbrushes 12, 113, **113**, 168
    techniques **108**, 113–14, 142
AJ Press books 177
Allied–Axis series 174
ammunition
    boxes **28**, 85
    packing crates 118
    racks 118
antennae and mounts 136, 153,
    154, 173
anti-slip plates **99**, 100
anti-tank guns: modelling 87–91,
    91
armament *see* guns; howitzers;
    machine guns
armour
    radiators 100
    scratch-building side skirts
        137–40, **139**
    thinning walls 106
Armour Modelling & Preservation
    Society 179
Arms and Armour Press books 177
assembly
    gluing techniques 18, 53–4,
        66–8, **88**
    Hotchkisses 106–9
Auto & Technik Museum 179
axes 140, **141**
axles 90

B

badges, personal 45
Baryatinsky, Mikhail 177
bases 48–59, 120, **121–2**, 149–50,
    149–51
    countryside 48–52, **48–51**, 120,
        121–2, 149–50, **149–51**
    levelling 53, **53**
    painting 48–9, 59
    townscape 52–9, **52–8**

types 48
beards and beard growth 45, **45–6**,
    46
Becker, Major Alfred 105
bending techniques
    metal 28, 60, 62, **65**, 68–9,
        69–70, **70**, 129
    plastic 22, **25**
    Plastruct I-beam 102
    styrene 133
    wire 65–6
bins *see* stowage
bolts **155**
books 175–8
Bovington Tank Museum 178
bows: Hotchkisses 106
braces, internal 109, 130, **134**
Bradford, George 92
Brass-Assist tool 62–5, **66**
brass shells and cases **28**
bricks **54**, 55–6
brushes 10–11, **11**–12
    brush-stroke direction 32
    for cement application 11
    cleaning 10–11
    stippling brushes 32
    techniques for painting with 32
    see also airbrushes
buckets **28**
buildings 52–8, **52–8**
    levelling 54–5
    painting **54**, 55–7, **56–7**
bushes *see* trees and bushes

C

cabs
    Deacons **90**
    half-tracks **97**, 98, 100
    StuGs 133, **136**
camouflage
    clothing 123–4, **124**, 149, **150**
    foliage 110, 117–19, 120
    painted 114, **115–16**, 128, 142
    winter whitewash 34, **34**
case catchers **20**
cast effect 106, 111, 154
casting: resin parts **131–2**, 131–2
casting numbers **26**
cements *see* glues
chassis

Deacons 87–90, **88**
    half-tracks **96–7**, 98
chips and scratches 40, **41**
chisels 43, 65
Choppers 129, **139**
close-quarters defence weapons 134
clothing and uniforms
    camouflage 123–4, **124**, 149,
        150
    painting 43–7, **44–7**, 123–4,
        124, 148–9, **150**
Cobbaton Combat Collection 178
cobblestones 56
compressors 113
Concord books 175
cupolas
    armoured deflectors **140**
    Tiger **20**, 30
    Tiran **154–5**
cushions 101
cutting mats **6**, 7

D

Darlington Publications books 176
Deacon anti-tank guns: modelling
    87–91, **91**
decals and markings
    dry transfer **169**, 170
    Free French M3A3 Stuarts 73
    half-tracks 103
    masks **61**
    painting 167–8, **167**
    preparation 167, **167**
    rubdown 36–7
    setting solution 143–4
    stencils 38–9, **40**
    Tiran 167–8, **167**, 169, **170**
    waterslide 30–1, 35–6, **37**,
        143–4
discussion groups 178
ditches **51**, 52
doors and doorframes
    buildings **56**, 57, 58
    Hotchkisses 109
Doyle, Hilary Louis 176
drills and bits 13
driver's areas: colours 22
driver's front plates
    fitting 22
    weathering 31

dry-brushing 24
dry-fitting 14

E

ejector-pin marks **15**, 17
  removing 16, 17–18
enamel paint 9–10, **10**
engine decks 108, 159, 160
engines
  air intakes 133
  Deacon 90
  exhaust gratings 110
  highlighting **36**
  M2 half-track **95–6**, 98
  Verlinden T-55 resin 159–67,
    162–3
etched-metal parts 60–73
  attaching **25**, 28–9, 66–8, 69
  bending 28, 60, 62, **65**, 68–9,
    69–70, **70**, 129
  bending rods or wire 65–6
  constructing fenders 129–30, **130**
  Eduard sets **60–1**, **93**, 99
  joining together 129
  masks **61**
  removing from frets **25**, 28, 66,
    68
  rolling 62–5, **66**, 69–70, **70**–1
  tools to use with 13, 62–6, **65–6**
  Voyager sets **62**
exhausts 20
  gratings 110
  painting 29, **29**, 35
  rear screens 66–8, **68**, 164
  stacks 132, **135**, 147
  StuG pipes 128
  thermal shield exhaust covers 163
eyebrows 46, **46**
eyes 45, **45–6**, 46, 123, **123**

F

faces: painting 43–6, **44–6**, 124–5,
  124–5, 148
fenders
  detailing 140, 159, 160
  making brass 129–30, **130**
  replacing with resin 159, **160**
  Tiran 159, 160, 171
fighting compartments 133, 134
figures 40–7, 120–5, 148–9
  altering heads 42, **42**
  clothing and uniforms 43–7,
    44–7

painting 43–7, **44**–7, 120-5,
  123–5, 148–9
  securing to bases 150
Filbert brushes 11
files 7, **7**
filler caps **83**
fillers **8**, 9
  using 17–18, 54–5, **155**, 160
FineScale Modeler (magazine) 174
fire extinguishers and mounts 89,
  140, **157**
flag mounts **157**
flame suppressor stacks 132, **135**
flash: removing 17, **154**
Flat brushes 11
flesh tones: painting 43–6, **44–6**,
  124–5, **124–5**, 148
Fletcher, David 177–8
floors
  broken wooden 57–8, **58**
  half-tracks **97**, 98, **99**, 100
foliage
  on bases 49–52, **49–51**, 120, **122**
  as camouflage 110, 117–19, 120
foot rails and supports 101
'frisket' 13
fuel drums and tanks
  cable releases **84**
  on Deacon **88**
  filler caps **83**
  fuel pipes and lines 83–4, 159,
    161
  on half-tracks **97**, 98, 101
  on tanks 79, **82–4**, 160, 169

G

gear levers: making 87, **87**
Geschützwagen: modelling 104–25,
  104–5
glacis plates: fitting 22
glues 7–9, **8**
  for etched metal 66–8
  for large parts 53–4
  mixing two-part **88**
  for resin parts 133, 152–3
  for small parts 159
  using 18
  for weight-bearing parts **87**
  see also superglue
grab handles: making 65–6, **67**,
  101, 103, **165**
grass 49–50, **49**, 50–2, 120, **122**,
  150, **151**

'greasy' feel: removing 11, 153
Ground Power series 175
groundwork 48, 120, **121–2**,
  149–50, **149–51**
grousers and racks 70, **72**
gun barrels
  assembly 26, 29–30
  colours 30
  filling sink marks 18
  removing flash 17
  replacing with metal 86–7
  retainers **27**
guns
  anti-tank **89**
  breech assembly 30
  case deflectors **79**
  colours **20**, 30, 85
  mounts 135–6, **136**
  StuG 135–6, **136**
  Tiran 152, **156**, 159
  weathering mantlets 172
  see also machine guns

H

hair 46, **46**
half-tracks
  etched sets **93**
  M2
    modelling 92–103, **102**
    scale plan **94–95**
  M3A1 92
  M3A2 kits 92, **93**
handles 133, 135
  grab handles 65–6, **67**, 101,
    103, **165**
hatches
  detailing 133, 134–5, **155**, 159,
    165
  engraving 133
  fitting 22
  making 134
  opening solid 85
  painting inner 170
  reconfiguring 133–4, **135**
  Tiger 22
  Tiran 154–5, 159, **162**, 170
headlamps
  attaching guards **80**
  guard covers **164**
  reflectors 33, **33**
  replacing solid lenses 64, **64**
  shaping guards 69
  wiring conduits **164**

heads
  altering 42, **42**
  painting 43–6, **44–6**, 124–5,
    124–5, 148
  resin **148**, 149
hinges 100, 133, 134, **155**
Histoire & Collections books 177
Hold and Fold bending tool **65**, 129
Hotchkiss Geschützwagen: modelling
  104–25
howitzers 110, 113
  armoured shields 109, **110**
  breeches and muzzle brakes 110
  wire camouflage screens 110, 113
hulls
  M3A1 Stuart 79
  Tiran 159, **160–1**
Hunnicutt, R. P. 92–8, 177

I

Ian Allan books 175, 177
ID plates **164**
Imperial War Museum 178
infrared searchlights 158
instruction sheets 14
instrument panels and dials
  Deacon **89**
  tanks 61, 85
International Plastic Modellers
  Society 179
Internet resources 178
interiors
  half-tracks 100–1, **102**
  Hotchkiss 106, **107**, 109,
    118–19
  Stuart 79–85, **86**
  Tiger 19, 22
IR searchlights **158**

J

jack securing clasps **24**
Jentz, Thomas 176, 177
jerrycans and holders **28**, 156–7,
  170

K

knives and blades 6–7, **6**, 128
Kubinka Tank Museum 179

L

lacquers 10, **10**
lamps and cables **80–1**

see also headlamps; infrared searchlights; taillights
Land Warfare Hall 178
lenses
  replacing solid lenses 64, **64**
  weathering 33
lights *see* headlamps; infrared searchlights; lamps and cables; taillights
loader's tool bins 161
location pins and holes 14
lockers 100–1
locking levers 135
logs 49, **49**

M

M2 half-track
  modelling 92–103, **102**
  scale plan **94**
M3A1 half-track 92
M3A1 Stuart: modelling 78–87,
  85
M3A2 half-track: kits 92, **93**
M3A3 Stuart: modelling 60–2,
  66–73
M14/41 **45**
machine guns
  assembly **26**, 29–30
  barrel colours 30
  half-tracks 103
  headpads 22, **25**
  replacing cradles and jackets 103
  rolling perforated outer jackets
    69
  skid mounts 100, 102–3
  StuG 133, **135**
  Tiran 152, **155**
magazines 174–5
magnifiers 45
markings *see* decals and markings
masking tape and sheet 13, **112**
masking techniques 18–22, **19**, **21**,
  112
masonry *see* buildings; walls
Matteliano, Tony 178
MBI books 177
Militärhistorisches Museum der
  Bundeswehr 179
Military Miniatures in Review (magazine)
  174
Military Modelcraft (magazine) 174
Military Modelling (magazine) 174,
  174
Military Vehicles Fotofax series 176

Milliput 8, 9
Missing Links website 178
Model Military International (magazine)
  174, **174**
modelling clubs 179
mortar 56–7
Motorbuch Verlag books 177
mould-release oils: removing 11,
  153
Muckleburgh Collection 178
mudflaps 140, 159, **164**
mufflers 110
Multi Tool rolling tool 65, 69
Munster Panzer Museum 178–9
Musée des Blindés 178
Museum Ordnance Specials 176
museums 178–9

N

Nahverteidigungswaffen 134
New Vanguard series 175, 177
Nuts & Bolts series 176

O

Osprey books 175, **175–7**

P

paint 9–11, **10**, 12, 43, **43**, 113–14
  mixing 22
  stirrers 12
  thinners 9–11, **10**
painting techniques
  airbrushing techniques **108**,
    113–14, **115–16**, 142
  base coats and undercoats 9,
    37–8, **38–9**, 168
  before assembly 15, 18–22
  brush-painting techniques 32
  camouflage 114, **115–16**, 128,
    142
  cast effect 106, 111, **154**
  chips and scratches
    using paint 40, 41, 114–19,
      145, 148
    using pencil 116, 119
    using salt mask **108**, 114
    using sponges 163, 168, **168**
  dry-brushing 24
  dust and mud effects
    using airbrushing 114,
      115–16
    using pastels 145, 167

using washes 31, 144–8, 170–2, **171**

figures 43–7, **44–7**, 120-5, **123–5**, 148–9

fine lines 12

handling models during 140, **142**

highlighting 35, **36**, 43–7, **44–7**, 117, 119–20, 124, **124**

Hotchkiss 106, 111–12, 114–20, **115–19**

masking 13, 18–22, **19**, **21**, 112

matching brush types to jobs 11–12

matching colours 12

metal effect 22, **30**

priming **38**, 140–2, 167

rust effect 29, **29**, 35

sand effect **171**, **172**

scale colour 39–40, 114

small parts **108**

spray paint techniques 12, 18–22

sprayed effect without airbrushes 32–3

stippling 29, 32

streaked effect 103, 114, 119

StuG 140–8, **142–7**

terrain 120, **121–2**

Tiran 152, 167–73, **167–72**

washes 144–8, **145**
  accent 124, **124**
  dust and mud effect with 31, 144–8, 170–2, **171**
  testing **19**
  weathering exteriors 31, 39–40, 114–20, **115–16**, 144–8, **144–7**, 170–3, **171**
  weathering interiors 85–6
  wet on wet 49
  winter whitewash 34, **34**
  wood varnish effect 34
  worn metal look **147**

Pansarmuseet 179

Panzer Tracts series **175**, 176

parts *see* etched-metal parts; plastic parts; resin parts; white-metal parts

periscopes
  colours **21**, 142
  tops and covers 133, **165**

Perth Military Modelling Site (PMMS) 178

pianos 58–9, **58**

pin vices and bits 13

plants 49–52, **49–51**, 120, **122**, 150, **151**

plastic card: working with 98-9

plastic parts
  bending 22, **25**
  identifying and matching up 14
  removing from sprues 15–17, **15**

Plastruct I-beam: bending 102

PMMS *see* Perth Military Modelling Site

pry bars 140

puddles 50

putties **8**, 9
  using 17–18, 54–5

R

radiators
  armour 100
  compartments: colours 22
  grilles and fans: colours 22
  hatch interiors **31**

radios
  aerials 69
  wiring **107**, 109

rear stowage baskets **70–1**

recuperator covers **109**

resin parts 74–87
  air bubbles 74, 77, 131
  attaching **79**
  casting 131–2, **131–2**
  combining with basic kits 153–73
  correcting warps 78
  fenders 159, **160**
  Formations sets **76**
  glues for 133, 152-3
  identifying 76, 153
  precautions 74, 153
  removing flash **154**
  removing from blocks 74–8, **75**
  repairing 78
  sanding 156, **162**
  shaping 78
  tools to use with 152

retaining devices **147**

Rigger brushes 11–12

rivets 99–100, 133, 134, 135, 138, **155**

rolling techniques 62–5, **66**, 69–70, **70–1**

rotary rasps 13

Round brushes 11–12

rubber 131

running gear 130–2
  see also tracks

S

sanding sticks 7, 152

saws and blades **6**

scale colour 39–40, 114

Scale Model Index website 178

Scale Models International (magazine) 174

scales: understanding 12

Schiffer Books publications 177

scrap boxes 128

screens 66–8, **68**, **82**, 85, **164**

scribing lines 98–9

seats 30, 85, 100, 101

shovels **139**

side cutters 15

side skirts
  painting 142–3, **143**, 146, 148
  scratch-building armoured 137–40, **139**

silvering 30, 35

sink marks *see* ejector-pin marks

sirens **80–1**

skid rails 102

skin tones: painting 43–6, **44–6**, 124–5, **124–5**, 148

smoke bombs and mortars **28**, 31

soldering tools and techniques 129–30, **130**

spares boxes 128

Spielberger, Walter 177

spray paint **10**, 12
  techniques 18–22

springs
  Deacon 90
  making 105, **105**, **135**, 140

sprockets and idlers **95**, 98

sprues
  identifying 14
  removing parts from 15–17, **15**
  stretched sprue 69

Squadron-Signal books 175–6

starter cranks 141

Steelmasters (magazine) 175

stencils 38–9, **40**

stippling 29, 32

stirrers 12

stonework 56, **56**

stowage
  half-track lockers 100–1
  loader's tool bins **161**

rear baskets 70–1
spare roadwheel bins 136
turret bins 27, 157–8
streams 50
stretched sprue 69
Sturmgeschütz IV: modelling
126–51
styrene sheet and strip 128
bending 133
cutting 129
sump protector supports 96
superglue 9
debonding 68
using 67–8, 69
suspension
assembly 18
Deacon 90
fixed vs movable 18
half-tracks 95, 98
Hotchkiss 105–6, 106
painting 18–22, 19
torsion bars 17

T
taillights 103
Tamiya Model Magazine International
174
tank modelling
M3A1 Stuart 78–87, 85
M3A3 Stuart 60–2, 66–73
M14/41 45
Tiger 14–31
Tiran 152–73
tank destroyer modelling: StuG
126–51
Tanks Illustrated series 176
tarps 118
teeth 46, 46
terrain: making and painting 120,
121–2
thermal shield exhaust covers 163
tie-downs 68, 69
making 65–6, 67, 101, 103,
157–8, 159
Tiran 5 MBT
colours 152
history 152
modelling 152–73
Tiger: modelling 14–31
tools, tank
clamps and straps 68–9, 140, 141
Hotchkiss 111
painting 29, 34, 142

stowage brackets 140, 141
see also individual tools by name
torsion bars 17, 160
tow cables
locks and lifting eyes 164
painting 169
shackles and hooks 27, 170
trackguards
making for half-tracks 103
thinning ends 35
weathering 31
Tiger 24–9
Track-Link website 178
tracks
assembling 21, 22–4, 80
attaching 106
highlighting 36
Hotchkiss 105–6
Modelkasten 63, 63
painting and weathering 24, 144,
166
rubber pads 24
spare track bars 136
spare track racks 70, 73
StuG 130, 132, 141
T-55 166, 166
troubleshooting 63
WWII Productions 166, 166
Trackstory books 176-7
trailer connection points 103
treadplates 129–30, 130
trees and bushes 49–51, 50–2, 150,
151
turrets
colours 20, 30
grousers and racks 70, 72
M3A3 Stuart 70, 72
painting 21
stowage bins 27, 157–8
Tiran 153–9, 154–8
tweezers 7
tyres
painting 21, 22, 142, 146
simulating damage 35
tidying up and attaching 91

U
uniforms *see* clothing and uniforms

V
Vanguard series 175
vegetation 49–52, 49–51, 120,
122, 150, 151

Verlinden books 176
vignettes 48–59, 120–5, 148–51

W
walls
masonry 120, 121–2
thinning armoured 106
see also buildings
War Machines series 176
water effect 50
water reservoirs and hoses 165
watercolour paint 43
websites 178
Wehrtechnische Studiensammlung
179
weld beads: making 109, 111,
159
wheels
assembly 18
bins for spares 136
Deacons 90–1
painting 18–22, 19, 21, 166
T-55 166, 166
weathering 31
white-metal parts 87
windows and frames 55–6, 57, 58
winter whitewash 34, 34
wire
bending 65–6
buying 66
straightening 81
wire cutters 29, 66
wiring: radios 107, 109
wiring harness 28
wood
broken floors 57–8, 58
doors and frames 56, 57, 58
varnish effect 34
windows and frames 55–6, 57,
58

X
Xtreme Modelling (magazine) 175

Y
Yahoo discussion groups 178

Z
Zaloga, Steven J. 98, 177
Zimmerit anti-magnetic paste 128,
146
simulating 129, 136–7, 137–8